Golf Rules Finder

Books by Scott Pickard:

Due Diligence List

Olympic Fusion

Golf Rules Finder

Scott S. Pickard

Due Diligence List
Olympic Fusion

iUniverse, Inc.
New York Lincoln Shanghai

Golf Rules Finder

Copyright © 2006 by Scott S. Pickard

iUniverse books may be ordered through booksellers or by contacting:

iUniverse
2021 Pine Lake Road, Suite 100
Lincoln, NE 68512
www.iuniverse.com
1-800-Authors (1-800-288-4677)

Golf Rules Finder is designed to be an easy-navigation golf rules lookup book that golfers can carry with them in their bag. Each rule is broken down into keywords and phrases cross-referenced so that the golfer can find the relevant rule fast. Diagrams are included for common relief procedures.

This book is based on the *Rules of Golf* and *The Decisions on the Rules of Golf* (2006–2007) which are published by the Royal and Ancient Golf Club of St. Andrews and the United States Golf Association, all rights reserved. In case of doubt, readers should refer to the full text of the *Rules and Decisions* as published in the official publications.

ISBN-13: 978-0-595-40142-0 (pbk)
ISBN-13: 978-0-595-84522-4 (ebk)
ISBN-10: 0-595-40142-2 (pbk)
ISBN-10: 0-595-84522-3 (ebk)

Printed in the United States of America

To Mom and Dad, who,
First, taught me to respect the game as a caddie, and,
Second, taught me to love the game as a player.

The Rules of Golf

A

Abandon provisional ball

- *Provisional Ball*

Abnormal conditions

- *Committee*

Abnormal Ground Conditions (Rule 25–1)

- Definition: An *abnormal ground condition* is any casual water, ground under repair or hole, cast or runway on the course made by a burrowing animal, a reptile or a bird.

Interference

- Definition: Interference by an abnormal ground condition occurs when a ball lies in or touches the condition or when the condition interferes with the player's stance or the area of his intended swing. If the player's ball lies on the <u>putting green</u>, interference also occurs if an abnormal ground condition on the putting green intervenes on his line of putt. Otherwise, intervention on the line of play is not, of itself, interference under this Rule.

- Local Rule: The Committee may make a Local Rule denying the player relief from interference with his stance by an abnormal ground condition.

Relief

- Except when the ball is in a water hazard or a lateral water hazard, a player may take relief from interference by an abnormal ground condition as follows:

    (i) <u>Through the Green</u>: If the [1—**ball lies through the green**], the player must <u>lift the ball</u> and [4—**drop it without penalty within one club-length**] of and [2—**not nearer the hole**] than the [3—**nearest point of relief**]. The nearest point of relief must not be in a hazard or on a putting green. When the ball is dropped within one club-length of the nearest point of relief, the ball must first strike a part of the course at a spot that avoids interference by the condition and is not in a hazard and not on a putting green.

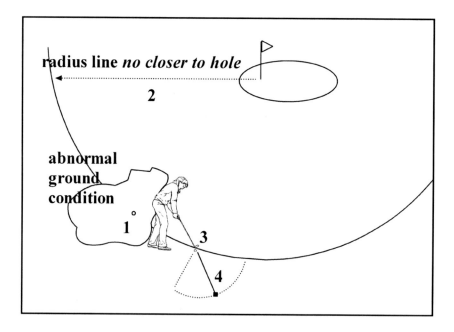

    (ii) <u>In a Bunker</u>: If the [1—**ball is in a bunker**], the player must lift the ball and drop it either:

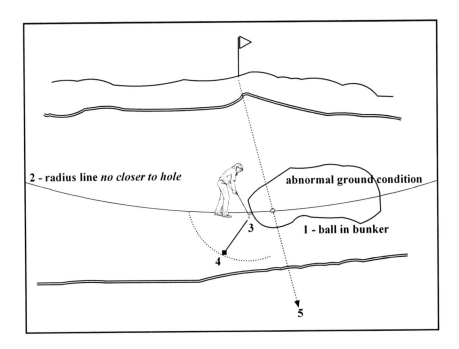

(a) <u>Without penalty</u>, in accordance with Clause (i) above, except that the [3—**nearest point of relief**] must be in the bunker and the [4—**ball must be dropped in the bunker one-club length**] from 3; or if complete relief is impossible, as near as possible to the spot where the ball lay, but [2—**not nearer the hole**], on a part of the course in the bunker that affords maximum available relief from the condition; or

(b) <u>Under penalty of one stroke</u>, [5—**outside the bunker**], keeping the point where the ball lay directly between the hole and the spot on which the ball is dropped, with no limit to how far behind the bunker the ball may be dropped.

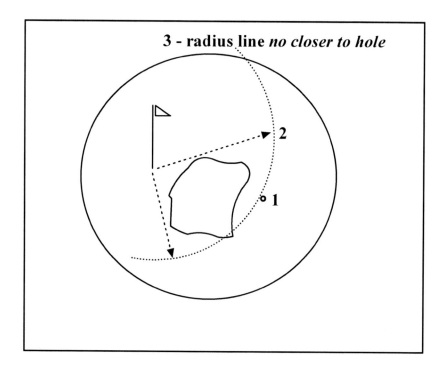

3 - radius line *no closer to hole*

(iii) <u>On the Putting Green</u>: If the [**1—ball lies on the putting green**], the player must lift the ball and place it without penalty at the [**2—nearest point of relief that is not in a hazard**], or if complete relief is impossible, at the nearest position to where it lay that affords maximum available relief from the condition, but [**3—not nearer the hole**] and not in a hazard. The nearest point of relief or maximum available relief may be off the putting green.

(iv) <u>On the Teeing Ground</u>: If the ball lies on the teeing ground, the player must lift the ball and drop it without penalty in accordance with Clause (i) above.

- <u>Clean ball</u>: The ball may be cleaned when lifted.

- <u>Ball rolls</u>: If the ball rolls to a position where there is interference by the condition from which relief was taken, see Rule *Dropping and Re-Dropping*.

- <u>Exception</u>: A player may not take relief under this Rule if:

(a) it is clearly unreasonable for him to make a stroke because of interference by anything other than an abnormal ground condition; or,

(b) interference by an abnormal ground condition would occur only through use of an unnecessarily abnormal stance, swing or direction of play.

- <u>Water hazard</u>: If a ball is in a water hazard (including a lateral water hazard), the player is not entitled to relief without penalty from interference by an abnormal ground condition. The player must play the ball as it lies (unless prohibited by Local Rule) or proceed under Rule *Relief for Ball in Water Hazard.*

- <u>Ball not recoverable</u>: If a ball to be dropped or placed under this Rule is not immediately recoverable, another ball may be substituted.

Ball Lost

- <u>Reasonable evidence</u>: It is a question of fact whether a ball lost after having been struck toward an abnormal ground condition is lost in such a condition. In order to treat the ball as lost in the abnormal ground condition, there must be reasonable evidence to that effect. In the absence of such evidence, the ball must be treated as a lost ball and Rule *Ball Lost or Out of Bounds* applies.

- If a ball is lost in an abnormal ground condition, the spot where the ball last crossed the outermost limits of the condition must be determined and, for the purpose of applying this Rule, the ball is deemed to lie at this spot and the player may take relief as follows:

  (i) <u>Through the Green</u>: If the ball last crossed the outermost limits of the abnormal ground condition at a spot through the green, the player may substitute another ball without penalty and take relief as prescribed in *Relief—Through the Green* above.

(ii) <u>In a Bunker</u>: If the ball last crossed the outermost limits of the abnormal ground condition at a spot in a bunker, the player may substitute another ball without penalty and take relief as prescribed in *Relief—In a Bunker* above.

(iii) <u>In a Water Hazard</u> (including a Lateral Water Hazard): If the ball last crossed the outermost limits of the abnormal ground condition at a spot in a water hazard, the player is not entitled to relief without penalty. The player must proceed under Rule *Relief for Ball in Water Hazard*.

(iv) <u>On the Putting Green</u>: If the ball last crossed the outermost limits of the abnormal ground condition at a spot on the putting green, the player may substitute another ball without penalty and take relief as prescribed in *Relief—On the Putting Green* above.

- *Ball Lost or Out of Bounds*
- *By Player, Partner, Caddie or Equipment* (Ball at Rest Moved)
- *Dropping and Re-Dropping*
- *Embedded Ball*
- *Provisional Ball*
- *Searching for Ball*
- *Wrong Putting Green*

Abnormal stance, swing or direction of play

- *Immovable Obstruction*

Absence of a referee

- *Disputes and Decisions*

Absent competitor or partner

- *Best-Ball and Four-Ball Match Play*
- *Four-Ball Stroke Play*

Academic institutions

- *Use of Golf Skill or Reputation*

Accept compensation, expenses, golf equipment, payment, prize

- *Prizes*
- *Professionalism*
- *Use of Golf Skill or Reputation*

Accept physical assistance

- *Assistance* (Striking the Ball)

Acceptable Forms of Gambling

- *Gambling*

Accidentally...

Deflected or stopped (ball)
- *By Opponent, Caddie or Equipment in Match Play*
- *By Outside Agency*
- *By Player, Partner, Caddie or Equipment*

Knock ball off tee
- *Ball falling off the tee*

Moved (ball or ball-marker)
- *Lifting and Marking*
- *Placing and Replacing*
- *Repair of Hole Plugs, Ball Marks and Other Damage*

- *Searching for Ball*
- *Three-Ball Match Play*

Act in appropriate manner

- *Other Conduct Incompatible with Amateurism*

Action to influence position or movement of ball

- *Exerting Influence on Ball*

Actual expenses

- *Use of Golf Skill or Reputation*

Addition of clubs

- *Maximum of 14 Clubs*

Addition of scores

- *Committee*
- *Stroke Play*

Addressing the Ball

- <u>Definition</u>: A player has *addressed the ball* when he has taken his stance and has also grounded his club. In a <u>hazard</u>, a player has addressed the ball when he has taken his stance.

- *Ball falling off the tee*
- *Ball in hazard*

- *By Player, Partner, Caddie or Equipment* (Ball at Rest Moved)

Adjustable clubs

- *Clubs*

Advantage

- *Playing from Wrong Place*
- *Playing out of turn*

Adversely affects opponent

- *Best-Ball and Four-Ball Match Play*

Advertise

- *Expenses*
- *Use of Golf Skill or Reputation*

Advice (Rule 8–1)

- <u>Definition</u>: *Advice* is any counsel or suggestion that could influence a player in determining his play, the choice of a club or the method of making a stroke. Information on the Rules or on matters of public information, such as the position of hazards or the flagstick on the putting green, is not advice.

- <u>Must Not Give or Ask</u>: During a stipulated round, a player must not:

    (a) give advice to anyone in the competition playing on the course other than his partner; or,

(b) ask for advice from anyone other than his partner or either of their caddies.

- *Indicating Line of Play*

Advisory opinion

- *Procedure for Enforcement of the Rules*

Affecting play

- *Artificial Devices and Unusual Equipment*

After competition closed

- *Disputes and Decisions*

After the player has begun the stroke

- *Playing Moving Ball*

Agent

- *Expenses*
- *Professionalism*

Agreement to discontinue play

- *Discontinuance of Play; Resumption of Play*

Agreement to Waive Rules (Rule 1–3)

- <u>Must not exclude or waive</u>: Players must not agree to exclude the operation of any Rule or to waive any penalty incurred.

- <u>Penalty for Breach of Rule</u>: *Match play*, Disqualification of both sides; *Stroke play*, Disqualification of competitors concerned.

- *Best-Ball and Four-Ball Match Play*
- *Bogey and Par Competitions*
- *Disputes and Decisions*
- *Four-Ball Stroke Play*
- *Game*
- *Stableford Competitions*

Agreement with a professional agent or sponsor

- *Professionalism*

Aiming (club)

- *Clubhead*

Alignment of club

- *Clubs*

All square

- *Match Play*

Allow to be improved

- *Improving Lie, Area of Intended Stance or Swing, or Line of Play*

Alteration of clubs

- *Clubs*
- *Damaged Clubs*

Alteration of Scorecard

- *Stroke Play*

Altered Lie

- *Ball Moved in Measuring* (Ball at Rest Moved)
- *Placing and Replacing*

Alternate play

- *Threesomes and Foursomes*

Amateur Status (Rules of Amateur Status)

- <u>Definition</u>: An *amateur golfer* is one who plays the game as a non–remunerative and non–profit–making sport and who does not receive remuneration for teaching golf or for other activities because of golf skill or reputation, except as provided in the Rules.

- *Amateurism*
- *Conduct Detrimental to Golf*
- *Expenses*
- *Gambling*
- *Instruction*
- *Procedure for Enforcement of the Rules*
- *Professionalism*
- *Prizes*
- *Use of Golf Skill or Reputation*
- *Reinstatement of Amateur Status*

Amateurism

- <u>Amateur Status</u>: Amateur status is a universal condition of eligibility for playing in golf competitions as an amateur golfer. A person who acts contrary to the Rules may forfeit his status as an amateur golfer and as a result will be ineligible to play in amateur competitions.

- <u>Doubt as to Rules and Appeal Process</u>: Any person who considers that any action he is proposing to take might endanger his amateur status may submit particulars to the staff of the United States Golf Association for an advisory opinion. If dissatisfied with the staff's advisory opinion, he may, by written notice to the staff within 30 days after being notified of the advisory opinion, appeal to the Amateur Status and Conduct Committee, in which case he shall be given reasonable notice of that Committee's next meeting at which the matter may be heard and shall be entitled to present his case in person or in writing. In such cases the staff shall submit to the Committee all information provided by the player together with staff's findings and recommendation, and the Amateur Status and Conduct Committee shall issue a decision on the matter. If dissatisfied with the Amateur Status and Conduct Committee's decision, the player may, by written notice to the staff within 30 days after being notified of the decision, appeal to the Executive Committee, in which case he shall be given reasonable notice of the next meeting of the Executive Committee at which the matter may be heard and shall be entitled to present his case in person or in writing. The decision of the Executive Committee shall be final.

- *Amateur Status*
- *Gambling*

Amount of money involved

- *Gambling*

Angle of club lie

- *Clubhead*

Announce decision

- *Committee*

Announce in advance

- *Doubt as to Procedure* (stroke play)

Announce match time

- *Committee*

Announced results

- *Disputes and Decisions*

Another Ball in Motion

- *Making Stroke While Another Ball in Motion*

Another Form of Match Played Concurrently

- *Best-Ball and Four-Ball Match Play*

Appeal Process

- *Amateurism*
- *Committee Decision*

- *Disputes and Decisions*
- *Procedure for Enforcement of the Rules*
- *Reinstatement of Amateur Status*

Appearance

- *Use of Golf Skill or Reputation*

Appendages (club)

- *Clubhead*

Application of foreign material to the club face

- *Foreign Material*

Application of the handicap

- *Stroke Play*

Applications for Reinstatement

- *Reinstatement of Amateur Status*

Apply handicap

- *Committee*

Applying for a professional's position

- *Professionalism*

Appointed by the Committee

- *Disputes and Decisions*

Approved by the USGA

- *Use of Golf Skill or Reputation*

Area of Intended Stance or Swing

- *Abnormal Ground Conditions*
- *Improving Lie, Area of Intended Stance or Swing, or Line of Play*

Area on which players may practice

- *Committee*

Arrange the date of their match

- *Committee*

Arrives at starting point

- *Time of Starting and Groups*

Articles

- *Use of Golf Skill or Reputation*

Artificial Devices & Unusual Equipment (Rule 14–3)

- <u>USGA Can change the Rules</u>: The United States Golf Association (USGA) reserves the right, at any time, to change the Rules relating to artificial devices and unusual equipment and make or change the interpretations relating to these Rules.

- <u>Manufacturer may submit a sample item</u>: A manufacturer may submit to the USGA a sample of an item to be manufactured for a ruling as to whether its use during a stipulated round would cause a player to be in breach of the Rule. The sample becomes the property of the USGA for reference purposes. If a manufacturer fails to submit a sample before manufacturing and/or marketing the item, the manufacturer assumes the risk of a ruling that use of the item would be contrary to the Rules.

- <u>Player must not use any artificial device</u>: Except as provided in the Rules, during a stipulated round the player must not use any artificial device or unusual equipment:

  (a) That might assist him in making a stroke or in his play; or,

  (b) For the purpose of gauging or measuring distance or conditions that might affect his play; or,

  (c) That might assist him in gripping the club, except that:

    (i)   plain gloves may be worn;

    (ii) resin, powder and drying or moisturizing agents may be used; and

    (iii) a towel or handkerchief may be wrapped around the grip.

- <u>Penalty for Breach of Rule</u>: Disqualification.

- *Best-Ball and Four-Ball Match Play*
- *Bogey and Par Competitions*
- *Four-Ball Stroke Play*

- *Stableford Competitions*
- *Striking the Ball*

Artificial Objects

- Obstruction: Is an *Obstruction* if it is not an integral part of the course.

- *Obstructions*

Ask for advice

- *Advice*

Ask opponent

- *Stroke*

Asked to lift ball

- *Ball Interfering with Play*

Assistance (Rule 14–2)

- A player must not: In making a stroke, a player must not:

    (a) Accept physical assistance or protection from the elements; or,

    (b) Allow his caddie, his partner or his partner's caddie to position himself on or close to an extension of the line of play or the line of putt behind the ball.

- Penalty for Breach of Rule: *Match Play*, Loss of hole; *Stroke Play*, Two strokes.

- *Artificial Devices and Unusual Equipment*
- *Ball Assisting Play*
- *Caddie*
- *Repair of Hole Plugs, Ball Marks and Other Damage*
- *Striking the Ball*

Assistant professional

- *Professionalism*

Assists partner

- *Best-Ball and Four-Ball Match Play*
- *Four-Ball Stroke Play*

Association of Intercollegiate Athletics for Women

- *Use of Golf Skill or Reputation*

Astride

- *Standing Astride or on Line of Putt*

At Rest (ball)

- *By Another Ball*

Attachments

- *Clubs*
- *Shaft*

Attended (flagstick)

- *Flagstick Attended, Removed or Held Up*

Auction sweepstakes

- *Gambling*

Author of the commentary, articles or books

- *Use of Golf Skill or Reputation*

Authority

- *Reinstatement of Amateur Status*

Authorized to attend flagstick

- *Flagstick Attended, Removed or Held Up*

Authorized

By USGA
- *Committee*

To pay expenses
- *Expenses*

Avoiding interference with stance

- *Tee-Markers*

Awaiting Reinstatement

- *Reinstatement of Amateur Status*

Awards

- *Prizes*

Axis (grip)

- *Grip*

B

Back

- *Clubhead*

Backstroke

- *Ball in Hazard*

Backward movement of the club

- *Improving Lie, Area of Intended Stance or Swing, or Line of Play*

Bad lie

- *Ball Played as it Lies*

Bad weather

- *Discontinuance of Play; Resumption of Play*

Bag

- DON'T place it on the green.

- *Clubs*

Ball

- <u>Mark ball</u>: The responsibility for playing the proper ball rests with the player. Each player should put an identification mark on his ball (Rule *Mark the ball*). (**Rule 6–5**)

- <u>Ball must conform</u>: The ball the player uses must conform to requirements specified in Appendix III, *The Ball*. The *Committee* may require, in the conditions of a competition, that the ball the player plays must be named on the current "List of Conforming Golf Balls" issued by the United States Golf Association. (**Rule 5–1**)

- *Ball Unfit for Play*
- *Foreign Material*
- *Mark the ball*
- *The Ball*
- *The Player*

Ball Assisting Play (Rule 22–1)

- <u>Lift the ball</u>: Except when a ball is in motion, if a player considers that a ball might assist any other player, he may:

  (a) lift the ball if it is his ball, or

  (b) have any other ball lifted.

- <u>Replace and NOT clean</u>: A ball lifted under this Rule must be replaced (see Rule *Placing and Replacing*). The ball must not be cleaned unless it lies on the putting green (see Rule *Cleaning Ball*).

- <u>Play before lift option</u>: In stroke play, a player required to lift his ball may play first rather than lift the ball.

- <u>Disqualification</u>: In stroke play, if the Committee determines that competitors have agreed not to lift a ball that might assist any other player, they are disqualified.

- *Ball Interfering with Play*

Ball at Rest Moved (Rule 18)

Ball at Rest Moved (Rule 18)	Ball in Motion Deflected or Stopped (Rule 19)
By Outside Agency	*By Outside Agency*
By Player, Partner, Caddie, or Equipment	*By Player, Partner, Caddie, or Equipment*
By Opponent, Caddie or Equipment in Match Play	*By Opponent, Caddie or Equipment in Match Play*
By Fellow-Competitor, Caddie, or Equipment in Stroke Play	*By Fellow-Competitor, Caddie, or Equipment in Stroke Play*
By Another Ball	*By Another Ball*
Ball Moved in Measuring	

- *Playing Moving Ball*
- *Three-Ball Match Play*

Ball breaks into pieces

- *Ball Unfit for Play*

Ball cleaned

- *Cleaning Ball*
- *Movable Obstruction*

Ball Comes to Rest in Same or Another Water Hazard

- *Ball Played Within Water Hazard*

Ball covered

- *Searching for Ball*

Ball Deemed to Move

- *Move or Moved*

Ball dropped

- *Dropping and Re-Dropping*
- *When Ball Dropped or Placed is in Play*

Ball embedded

- *Embedded Ball*

Ball Fails to Come to Rest

- *Placing and Replacing*

Ball Falling Off Tee (Rule 11–3)

- <u>Re-tee without penalty</u>: If a ball, when not in play, falls off a tee or is knocked off a tee by the player in addressing it, it may be re–teed without penalty.

- Stroke counts: However, if a stroke is made at the ball in these circumstances, whether the ball is moving or not, the stroke counts but there is no penalty.

- *Playing Moving Ball*
- *Teeing Ground*

Ball falls to pieces as you stroke it

- *Unfit for Play*

Ball farthest from the hole

- *Order of Play—Stroke Play*

Ball Holed

- *Holed*

Ball identification

- *Identifying your ball*

Ball in Hazard; Prohibited Actions (Rule 13–4)

- Player must not: Before making a stroke at a ball that is in a hazard (whether a bunker or a water hazard) or that, having been lifted from a hazard, may be dropped or placed in the hazard, the player must not:

  (a) Test the condition of the hazard or any similar hazard.

  (b) Touch the ground in the hazard or water in the water hazard with his hand or a club (*grounding club*).

(c) Touch or move a loose impediment lying in or touching the hazard.

- Exceptions:

  1. Provided nothing is done that constitutes testing the condition of the hazard or improves the lie of the ball, there is no penalty if the player:

     (a) touches the ground in any hazard or water in a water hazard: (i) as a result of or to prevent falling; (ii) in removing an obstruction; (iii) in measuring or in retrieving, lifting, placing or replacing a ball under any Rule; or,

     (b) places his clubs in a hazard.

  2. After making the stroke, the player or his caddie may smooth sand or soil in the hazard, provided that, if the ball is still in the hazard or has been lifted from the hazard and may be dropped or placed in the hazard, nothing is done that improves the lie of the ball or assists the player in his subsequent play of the hole.

- <u>Player may touch with a club</u>: At any time, including at address or in the backward movement for the stroke, the player may touch with a club or otherwise any obstruction, any construction declared by the Committee to be an integral part of the course or any grass, bush, tree or other growing thing.

- <u>Penalty for Breach of Rule</u>: *Match Play*, Loss of hole; *Stroke Play*, Two strokes.

- *Ball Played as It Lies*
- *Hazard*
- *Relief for Ball in Water Hazard*

Ball in Motion Deflected or Stopped (Rule 19)

Ball at Rest Moved (Rule 18)	Ball in Motion Deflected or Stopped (Rule 19)
By Outside Agency	*By Outside Agency*
By Player, Partner, Caddie, or Equipment	*By Player, Partner, Caddie, or Equipment*
By Opponent, Caddie or Equipment in Match Play	*By Opponent, Caddie or Equipment in Match Play*
By Fellow-Competitor, Caddie, or Equipment in Stroke Play	*By Fellow-Competitor, Caddie, or Equipment in Stroke Play*
By Another Ball	*By Another Ball*
Ball Moved in Measuring	

- *Making Stroke While Another Ball in Motion*
- *Movable Obstruction*

Ball in Play

- <u>Definition</u>: A ball is *in play* as soon as the player has made a stroke on the teeing ground. It remains in play until it is holed, except when it is lost, out of bounds or lifted, or another ball has been substituted whether or not the substitution is permitted; a ball so substituted becomes the ball in play.

  <u>Outside teeing ground</u>: If a ball is played from outside the teeing ground when the player is starting play of a hole, or when attempting to correct this mistake, the ball is not in play and Rule *Playing from Outside Teeing Ground* or *Playing from Wrong Place* applies. Otherwise, ball in play includes a ball played from outside the teeing ground when the player elects or is required to play his next stroke from the teeing ground. <u>Exception in match play</u>: Ball in

play includes a ball played by the player from outside the teeing ground when starting play of a hole if the opponent does not require the stroke to be canceled in accordance with Rule *Playing from Outside Teeing Ground.*

- *Provisional Ball*
- *Substituted Ball*
- *When Ball Dropped or Placed is in Play*

Ball in Water Hazard

- *Relief for Ball in Water Hazard*

Ball Incorrectly Substituted, Dropped or Placed

- *Lifting Ball Incorrectly Substituted, Dropped or Placed*
- *When Ball Dropped or Placed is in Play*

Ball Interfering with Play (Rule 22–2)

- <u>May have ball lifted</u>: Except when a ball is in motion, if a player considers that the ball of another player might interfere with his play, he may have it lifted. In *stroke play*, a player required to lift his ball may play first rather than lift the ball.

- <u>Must be asked to lift ball</u>: Except on the putting green, a player may not lift his ball solely because he considers that it might interfere with the play of another player. If a player lifts his ball without being asked to do so, he incurs a penalty of one stroke for a breach of Rule *By Player, Partner, Caddie or Equipment*, but there is no additional penalty under this Rule.

- <u>Ball must be replaced</u>: A ball lifted under this Rule must be replaced (see Rule *Placing and Replacing*). The ball must not be cleaned unless it lies on the putting green (see Rule *Cleaning Ball*).

- <u>Penalty for Breach of Rule</u>: *Match play*, Loss of hole; *Stroke play*, Two strokes.

- *Ball Assisting Play*

Ball is in motion

- *Loose Impediments*

Ball lies in a hazard

- *Loose Impediments*

Ball lifted and/or cleaned

- *Ball Assisting Play*
- *Ball Interfering with Play*
- *Lifting Ball When Play Discontinued*
- *Movable Obstruction*
- *Relief for Ball in Water Hazard*

Ball Lost

- *Abnormal Ground Conditions*
- *Ball Lost in Obstruction*
- *Ball Played Within Water Hazard*
- *Lost Ball*
- *Provisional Ball*
- *Relief for Ball in Water Hazard*

Ball Lost in Obstruction (Rule 24–3)

- Reasonable evidence: It is a question of fact whether a ball lost after having been struck toward an obstruction is lost in the obstruction. In order to treat the ball as lost in the obstruction, there must be reasonable evidence to that effect. In the absence of such evidence, the ball must be treated as a lost ball and Rule *Ball Lost or Out of Bounds; Provisional Ball* applies.

Ball Lost in Movable Obstruction

- Drop with no penalty: If a ball is lost in a movable obstruction, a player may, without penalty, remove the obstruction and must through the green or in a hazard drop a ball, or on the putting green place a ball, as near as possible to the spot directly under the place where the ball last crossed the outermost limits of the movable obstruction, but not nearer the hole.

Ball Lost in Immovable Obstruction

- Relief: If a ball is lost in an immovable obstruction, the spot where the ball last crossed the outermost limits of the obstruction must be determined and, for the purpose of applying this Rule, the ball is deemed to lie at this spot and the player may take relief as follows:

  (i) Through the Green: If the ball last crossed the outermost limits of the immovable obstruction at a spot through the green, the player may substitute another ball without penalty and take relief as prescribed in Rule *Immovable Obstruction*.

  (ii) In a Bunker: If the ball last crossed the outermost limits of the immovable obstruction at a spot in a bunker, the player may substitute another ball without penalty and take relief as prescribed in Rule *Immovable Obstruction*.

  (iii) In a Water Hazard (including a Lateral Water Hazard): If the ball last crossed the outermost limits of the immovable obstruction at a spot in a water hazard, the player is not entitled to relief without penalty. The player must proceed under Rule *Relief for Ball in Water Hazard*.

(iv) <u>On the Putting Green</u>: If the ball last crossed the outermost limits of the immovable obstruction at a spot on the putting green, the player may substitute another ball without penalty and take relief as prescribed in Rule *Immovable Obstruction*.

- <u>Penalty for Breach of Rule</u>: *Match play*, Loss of hole; *Stroke play*, Two strokes.

- *Ball Lost or Out of Bounds*
- *Provisional Ball*

Ball Lost or Out of Bounds (Rule 27–1)

- <u>Stroke and distance</u>: If a ball is lost or is out of bounds, the player must play a ball, under penalty of one stroke, as nearly as possible at the spot from which the original ball was last played (see Rule *Making Next Stroke from Where Previous Stroke Made*).

Exceptions

1. <u>Water Hazard</u>: If there is reasonable evidence that the original ball is lost in a water hazard, the player must proceed in accordance with Rule *Relief for Ball in Water Hazard*.

2. <u>Obstruction</u> or <u>Abnormal Ground Conditions</u>: If there is reasonable evidence that the original ball is lost in an obstruction (Rule *Ball Lost in Obstruction*) or an abnormal ground condition (Rule *Abnormal Ground Conditions*) the player may proceed under the applicable Rule.

- <u>Penalty for Breach of Rule</u>: *Match play*, Loss of hole; *Stroke play*, Two strokes.

- *Provisional Ball*

Ball Lost or Unplayable Outside Hazard or Out of Bounds

- *Ball Played Within Water Hazard*

Ball Marker

- *Ball Moved in Measuring* (Ball at Rest Moved)
- *Lifting and Marking* (interferes with play)
- *Placing and Replacing*
- *Touching Line of Putt*

Ball Marks

- *Repair of Hole Plugs, Ball Marks and Other Damage*

Ball may be cleaned

- *Immovable Obstruction*

Ball moved

- *By Opponent, Caddie or Equipment in Match Play* (ball at rest moved)

Ball Moved in Measuring (Rule 18–6)

- <u>Ball/marker must be replaced</u>: If a ball or ball–marker is moved in measuring while proceeding under or in determining the application of a Rule, the ball or ball–marker must be replaced. There is no penalty provided the movement of the ball or ball–marker is directly attributable to the specific act of measuring.

- <u>Penalty for Breach of Rule</u>: *Match play*, Loss of hole; *Stroke play*, Two strokes.

- <u>Wrongly substituted ball</u>: If a player who is required to replace a ball fails to do so, he incurs the general penalty for breach of Rule. There is no additional penalty under this Rule, except in the case of a wrongly substituted ball (See *Substituted Ball*).

- <u>Ball not recoverable</u>: If a ball to be replaced under this Rule is not immediately recoverable, another ball may be substituted.

- <u>Lie altered</u>: If the original lie of a ball to be placed or replaced has been altered, see Rule *Placing and Replacing*.

- <u>Original spot not determined</u>: If it is impossible to determine the spot on which a ball is to be placed, see Rule *Placing and Replacing*.

- *Ball at Rest Moved*

Ball Moves

- <u>Definition</u>: Leaves its position and comes to rest in another place.

- *Dropping and Re-Dropping*
- *Movable Obstruction*
- *Placing and Replacing*
- *Playing Moving Ball*

Ball Moving in Water (Rule 14–6)

- <u>Player may make a stroke</u>: When a ball is moving in water in a water hazard, the player may, without penalty, make a stroke, but he must not delay making his stroke in order to allow the wind or current to improve the position of the ball.

- <u>Player may lift ball</u>: A ball moving in water in a water hazard may be lifted if the player elects to invoke Rule on *Water Hazard*.

- <u>Penalty for Breach of Rule</u>: *Match Play*, Loss of hole; *Stroke Play*, Two strokes.

- *Playing Moving Ball*
- *Relief for Ball in Water Hazard*
- *Striking the Ball*
- *Water Hazard*

Ball must be replaced

- *By Another Ball* (Ball at Rest Moved)

Ball Not Recoverable

- *Abnormal Ground Conditions*
- *Ball Moved in Measuring* (Ball at Rest Moved)
- *By Outside Agency*
- *Movable Obstruction*

Ball on the green

- *Putting Line*

Ball or ball-marker accidentally moved

- *Lifting and Marking*
- *Placing and Replacing*
- *Procedure When Play Resumed*
- *Repair of Hole Plugs, Ball Marks, and Other Damage*

Ball out of bounds

- *Provisional Ball*

Ball Overhanging Hole (Rule 16–2)

- <u>Allowed time to reach the hole plus 10 seconds</u>: When any part of the ball overhangs the lip of the hole, the player is allowed enough time to reach the hole without unreasonable delay and an additional ten seconds to determine whether the ball is at rest. If by then the ball has not fallen into the hole, it is deemed to be at rest.

- <u>Ball falls in hole after 10 seconds</u>: If the ball subsequently falls into the hole, the player is deemed to have holed out with his last stroke, and he must add a penalty stroke to his score for the hole.

- *Putting Green*
- *Undue Delay*

Ball paint is damaged or discolored

- *Ball Unfit for Play*

Ball Placed

- *When Ball Dropped or Placed is in Play*

Ball Played as It Lies (Rule 13)

- <u>Played as it lies</u>: The ball must be played as it lies, except as otherwise provided in the Rules. (Rule 13–1)

- *Ball in Hazard* (Prohibited Actions)
- *Building Stance*
- *Improving Lie, Area of Intended Stance or Swing, or Line of Play*

Ball Played Within Water Hazard (Rule 26–2)

Ball Comes to Rest in Same or Another Water Hazard

- Take relief: If a ball played from within a water hazard comes to rest in the same or another water hazard after the stroke, the player may:

  (i) proceed under Rule *Relief for Ball in Water Hazard*. If, after dropping in the hazard, the player elects not to play the dropped ball, he may:

  (a) with reference to this hazard, proceed under Rule *Relief for Ball in Water Hazard*, adding the additional penalty of one stroke prescribed by that Rule; or

  (b) add an additional penalty of one stroke and play a ball as nearly as possible at the spot from which the last stroke from outside a water hazard was made (see Rule *Making Next Stroke from Where Previous Stroke Made*); or

  (ii) proceed under Rule *Relief for Ball in Water Hazard*; or

  (iii) under penalty of one stroke, play a ball as nearly as possible at the spot from which the last stroke from outside a water hazard was made (see Rule *Making Next Stroke from Where Previous Stroke Made*).

Ball Lost or Unplayable Outside Hazard or Out of Bounds

- If a ball played from within a water hazard is lost or declared unplayable outside the hazard or is out of bounds, the player may, after taking a penalty of one stroke under Rule *Ball Lost or Out of Bounds* or *Ball Unplayable*:

  (i) play a ball as nearly as possible at the spot in the hazard from which the original ball was last played (see Rule *Making Next Stroke from Where Previous Stroke Made*); or

(ii) proceed under Rule *Relief for Ball in Water Hazard*, adding the additional penalty of one stroke prescribed by the Rule and using as the reference point the point where the original ball last crossed the margin of the hazard before it came to rest in the hazard; or

(iii) add an additional penalty of one stroke and play a ball as nearly as possible at the spot from which the last stroke from outside the hazard was made (see Rule *Making Next Stroke from Where Previous Stroke Made*).

- Not required to drop a ball: When proceeding under this Rule, the player is not required to drop a ball under Rule *Ball Lost or Out of Bounds* or *Ball Unplayable*. If he does drop a ball, he is not required to play it. He may alternatively proceed under this Rule (ii) or (iii) above.

- Ball unplayable: If a ball played from within a water hazard is declared unplayable outside the hazard, nothing in this Rule precludes the player from proceeding under Rule *Ball Unplayable*.

- Penalty for Breach of Rule: *Match play*, Loss of hole; *Stroke play*, Two strokes.

Ball purposely deflected or stopped

- *Playing Moving Ball*
- *Three-Ball Match Play*

Ball replaced and replayed

- *Unauthorized Attendance* (flagstick)

Ball Resting Against Flagstick (Rule 17–4)

- Player may move/remove flagstick: When the flagstick is in the hole and a player's ball when not holed rests against it, the player or another person authorized by him may move or remove the flag-stick, and if the ball falls into the hole, the player is deemed to have holed out with his last stroke; otherwise, the ball, if moved, must be placed on the lip of the hole, without penalty.

- *Flagstick*

Ball rolls

- *Abnormal Ground Conditions*
- *Immovable Obstruction*

Ball Striking Flagstick or Attendant (Rule 17–3)

- The player's ball must not strike:

    (a) The flagstick when it is being attended, removed or held up;

    (b) The person attending or holding up the flagstick; or

    (c) The flagstick in the hole, unattended, when the stroke has been made on the putting green.

- Exception: When the flagstick is attended, removed or held up without the player's authority (See *Unauthorized Attendance*).

- Penalty for Breach of Rule: *Match play*, Loss of hole; *Stroke play*, Two strokes and the ball must be played as it lies.

- *By Opponent, Caddie or Equipment in Match Play*
- *Flagstick*
- *Three-Ball Match Play*
- *Unauthorized Attendance* (flagstick)

Ball stuck in ground

- *Embedded Ball*

Ball substituted

- *Unfit for Play*

Ball surface is scratched or scraped

- *Ball Unfit for Play*

Ball touches something during drop

- *Dropping and Re-Dropping*

Ball Unfit for Play (Rule 5–3)

- <u>Cut, cracked, out of shape</u>: A ball is unfit for play if it is visibly cut, cracked or out of shape. A ball is not unfit for play solely because mud or other materials adhere to it, its surface is scratched or scraped or its paint is damaged or discolored.

- <u>Lift and examine</u>: If a player has reason to believe his ball has become unfit for play during play of the hole being played, he may lift the ball without penalty to determine whether it is unfit. Before lifting the ball, the player must announce his intention to his opponent in match play or his marker or a fellow–competitor in stroke play and mark the position of the ball. He may then lift and examine it provided that he gives his opponent, marker or fellow–competitor an opportunity to examine the ball and observe the lifting and replacement. The ball must not be cleaned when lifted. If the player fails to comply with all or any part of this procedure, he incurs a PENALTY of one stroke.

- <u>Substitute ball</u>: If it is determined that the ball has become unfit for play during play of the hole being played, the player may substitute another ball, placing it on the spot where the original ball lay. Otherwise, the original ball must be replaced.

- <u>Penalty for illegal substitution</u>: If a player substitutes a ball when not permitted and he makes a stroke at the wrongly substituted ball, he incurs the general penalty of: *Match play*, Loss of hole; *Stroke play*, Two strokes.

- <u>Ball breaks into pieces</u>: If a ball breaks into pieces as a result of a stroke, the stroke is canceled and the player must play a ball without penalty as nearly as possible at the spot from which the original ball was played (see *Making Next Stroke from Where Previous Stroke Made*).

- <u>Dispute</u>: If the opponent, marker or fellow–competitor wishes to dispute a claim of unfitness, he must do so before the player plays another ball.

- *Ball*
- *Cleaning Ball*
- *The Ball* (specifications)

Ball Unplayable (Rule 28)

- <u>Player sole judge</u>: The player may deem his ball unplayable at any place on the course except when the ball is in a water hazard. The player is the sole judge as to whether his ball is unplayable.

- <u>Penalty of one stroke</u>: If the player deems his ball to be unplayable, he must, under penalty of one stroke:

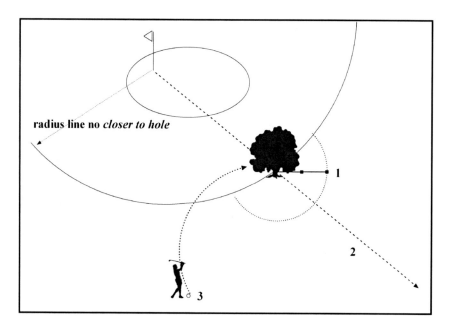

radius line no *closer to hole*

1—<u>Drop two club-lengths</u>: Drop a ball within two club-lengths of the spot where the ball lay, but not nearer the hole.

2—<u>Drop behind no limit</u>: Drop a ball behind the point where the ball lay, keeping that point directly between the hole and the spot on which the ball is dropped, with no limit to how far behind that point the ball may be dropped; or

3—<u>Play from original spot</u>: Play a ball as nearly as possible at the spot from which the original ball was last played (see Rule *Making Next Stroke from Where Previous Stroke Made*); or

- Bunker:

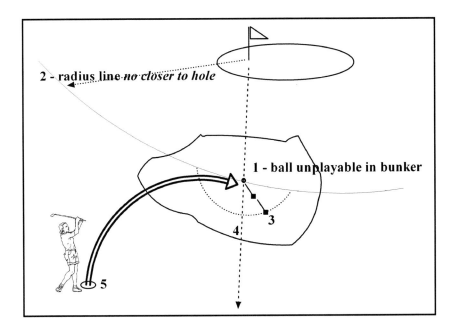

1—Ball comes to rest unplayable in a bunker.

2—Establish radius line *no closer to hole*.

3—Drop within 2-club lengths, no closer to hole, 1 penalty stroke; or

4—Drop INSIDE the bunker on the backwards extension of the line from the hole to the ball, 1 penalty stroke; or

5—Drop on the site of the last stoke, 1 penalty stroke.

- Lift and clean: The ball may be lifted and cleaned when proceeding under this Rule.

- Penalty for Breach of Rule: *Match play*, Loss of hole; *Stroke play*, Two strokes

Balls are equidistant from the hole

- *Order of Play—Match Play*

Be Ready to Play

- <u>Etiquette</u>: Players should be ready to play as soon as it is their turn to play. When playing on or near the putting green, they should leave their bags or carts in such a position as will enable quick movement off the green and towards the next tee. When the play of a hole has been completed, players should immediately leave the putting green.

Becoming a professional golfer

- *Professionalism*

Before a stroke

- *Tee-Markers*

Before Competition, Rounds, Practice

- *Practice*
- *Practice Before or Between Rounds*

Before the competition closed

- *Disputes and Decisions*

Behavior on the Course

- *Etiquette*

Bending grass, limbs, objects

- *Improving Lie, Area of Intended Stance or Swing, or Line of Play*
- *Searching for Ball*

Bending of shaft

- *Shaft*

Benefit

- *Use of Golf Skill or Reputation*

Bent shaft

- *Damaged Clubs*

Berries

- *Loose Impediments*

Best-Ball & Four-Ball Match Play (Rule 30–3)

- <u>Definition</u>: The lowest score in a three or four–man team (see *Better Ball*).

Representation of Side

- <u>Represented by one partner</u>: A side may be represented by one partner for all or any part of a match; all partners need not be present. An absent partner may join a match between holes, but not during play of a hole.

Maximum of 14 Clubs

- <u>Breach of rule by any partner</u>: The side is penalized for a breach of Rules *Damaged Clubs* and *Maximum of 14 Clubs* by any partner.

Order of Play

- <u>Side can choose</u>: Balls belonging to the same side may be played in the order the side considers best.

Wrong Ball

- <u>Disqualified for that hole</u>: If a player makes a stroke at a wrong ball that is not in a hazard, he is disqualified for that hole, but his partner incurs no penalty even if the wrong ball belongs to him. If the wrong ball belongs to another player, its owner must place a ball on the spot from which the wrong ball was first played.

Disqualification of Side

- <u>Breach of rule by any partner</u>: A side is disqualified for a breach of any of the following by any partner:

    Agreement to Waive Rules
    Artificial Devices and Unusual Equipment
    Caddie (more than one; failure to correct breach immediately)
    Clubs
    Handicap (playing off higher handicap)
    The Ball
    Undue Delay; Slow Play (repeated offense)

- <u>Breach of rule by all partners</u>: A side is disqualified for a breach of any of the following by all partners:

    Discontinuance of Play
    Time of Starting and Groups

- <u>Disqualified that hole only</u>: In all other cases where a breach of a Rule would result in disqualification, the player is disqualified for that hole only.

Effect of Other Penalties

- <u>Assists partner or adversely affects opponent</u>: If a player's breach of a Rule assists his partner's play or adversely affects an opponent's play, the partner incurs the applicable penalty in addition to any penalty incurred by the player.

- <u>Penalty does not apply to partner</u>: In all other cases where a player incurs a penalty for breach of a Rule, the penalty does not apply to his partner. Where the penalty is stated to be loss of hole, the effect is to disqualify the player for that hole.

Another Form of Match Played Concurrently

- <u>These rules apply</u>: In a best–ball or four–ball match when another form of match is played concurrently, the above specific Rules apply.

- *Match*
- *Three-Ball Match Play*

Better-Ball

- <u>Definition</u>: The lowest score in a two–man team.

- *Best-Ball and Four-Ball Match Play*
- *Committee* (score)

Betting

- *Gambling*

Between

Rounds (Practice)
- *Practice Before or Between Rounds*

Play of two holes
- *Practice During Round*

Blue stakes

- *Ground Under Repair*

Body (club)

- *Clubhead*

Bogey and Par Competitions (Rule 32–1a)

- <u>Scoring as in match play</u>: The scoring for bogey and par competitions is made as in match play. Any hole for which a competitor makes no return is regarded as a loss. The winner is the competitor who is most successful in the aggregate of holes. The marker is responsible for marking only the gross number of strokes for each hole where the competitor makes a net score equal to or less than the fixed score.

- <u>Maximum of 14 Clubs</u>: Penalties as in match play
  (see Rule *Maximum of 14 Clubs*).

- <u>One Caddie at Any One Time</u>: Penalties as in match play
  (see Rule *Caddie*).

- <u>Undue Delay; Slow Play</u>: The competitor's score is adjusted by deducting one hole from the overall result
  (see Rule *Undue Delay; Slow Play*).

Disqualification Penalties (Rule 32–2)

- From the Competition: (Rule 32–2a) A competitor is disqualified from the competition for a breach of any of the following:

  Agreement to Waive Rules
  Artificial Devices and Unusual Equipment
  Caddie
  (having more than one; failure to correct breach immediately)
  Clubs
  Discontinuance of Play
  Handicap
  (playing off higher handicap; failure to record handicap)
  Practice Before or Between Rounds
  Refusal to Comply with Rule
  Signing and Returning Scorecard
  The Ball
  Time of Starting and Groups
  Undue Delay; Slow Play (repeated offense)
  Wrong Score for Hole

- For a Hole: (Rule 32–2b) In all other cases where a breach of a Rule would result in disqualification, the competitor is disqualified only for the hole at which the breach occurred.

- *Stableford Competitions*

Bogey

- *Committee*

Books

- *Use of Golf Skill or Reputation*

Borrow any club

- *Clubs*
- *Damaged Clubs*
- *Maximum of 14 Clubs*

Boundary

- <u>In Bounds</u>: If the ball touches the boundary, it is *In Bounds*.

- *Committee*
- *Out of Bounds* (diagram)
- *Water Hazards*

Breach of Amateur Status

- *Procedure for Enforcement of the Rules*

Breach of etiquette

- *Committee*

Breach of the Rules

- *Best-Ball and Four-Ball Match Play*
- *Four-Ball Stroke Play*
- *General Penalty*
- *The Player*

Breaking limbs, anything growing or fixed

- *Improving Lie, Area of Intended Stance or Swing, or Line of Play*

Breaks into pieces (ball)

- *Ball Unfit for Play*

Broadcasting and Writing

- *Use of Golf Skill or Reputation*

Broken

- *Clubs*
- *Damaged Clubs*

Building Stance (Rule 13–3)

- <u>Must not build a stance</u>: A player is entitled to place his feet firmly in taking his stance, but he must not build a stance.

- *Ball Played as It Lies*
- *Improving Lie*
- *Stance*

Bulge

- *Grip*

Bunker

- <u>Definition</u>: A *bunker* is a hazard consisting of a prepared area of ground, often a hollow, from which turf or soil has been removed and replaced with sand or the like. Grass–covered ground bordering or within a bunker, including a stacked turf face (whether grass–covered or earthen), is not part of the bunker. A wall or lip of the bunker not covered with grass is part of the bunker. The margin of a bunker extends vertically downward, but not upward. A ball is in a bunker when it lies in or any part of it touches the bunker.

- DON'T ground your club.

- Etiquette: Before leaving a bunker, players should carefully fill up and smooth over all holes and footprints made by them and any nearby made by others. If a rake is within reasonable proximity of the bunker, the rake should be used for this purpose.

- *Abnormal Ground Conditions* (in a bunker)
- *Ball Lost in Obstruction*
- *Ball Unplayable*
- *Rakes*

Burrowing Animal

- Definition: A *burrowing animal* is an animal that makes a hole for habitation or shelter, such as a rabbit, mole, groundhog, gopher or salamander. A hole made by a non–burrowing animal, such as a dog, is not an *abnormal ground condition* unless marked or declared as ground under repair.

Business associate

- *Expenses*

By Another Ball

Ball at Rest Moved (Rule 18–5)

- Replace moved ball: If a ball in play and at rest is moved by another ball in motion after a stroke, the moved ball must be replaced (see *Ball at Rest Moved*).

Ball in Motion Deflected or Stopped (Rule 19–5)

- <u>At Rest</u>: If a player's ball in motion after a stroke is deflected or stopped by a ball in play and at rest, the player must play his ball as it lies. *Match play*, there is no penalty. *Stroke play*, there is no penalty unless both balls lay on the putting green prior to the stroke, in which case the player incurs a penalty of two strokes.

- <u>In Motion</u>: If a player's ball in motion after a stroke is deflected or stopped by another ball in motion after a stroke, the player must play his ball as it lies. There is no penalty unless the player was in breach of Rule *Making Stroke While Another Ball in Motion*, in which case he incurs the penalty for breach of that Rule.

- <u>Exception</u>: If the player's ball is in motion after a stroke on the putting green and the other ball in motion is an outside agency, see Rule *By Outside Agency*.

- <u>Penalty for Breach of Rule</u>: *Match play*, loss of hole; *Stroke play*, two strokes.

By Fellow-Competitor, Caddie or Equipment in Stroke Play

Ball moved, deflected, or stopped (Rule 18–4, 19–4)

- <u>No penalty</u>: If a fellow–competitor, his caddie or his equipment moves the player's ball, touches it or causes it to move, there is no penalty.

- <u>Must be replaced</u>: If the ball is moved, it must be replaced.

- *Ball at Rest Moved*
- *Ball in Motion Deflected or Stopped*
- *By Outside Agency*
- *Wrong Ball*

By Opponent, Caddie or Equipment in Match Play

Ball at Rest Moved (Rule 18–3)

- <u>During Search</u>: If, during search for a player's ball, an opponent, his caddie or his equipment moves the ball, touches it or causes it to move, there is no penalty. If the ball is moved, it must be replaced.

- <u>Other Than During Search</u>: If, other than during search for a player's ball, an opponent, his caddie or his equipment moves the ball, touches it purposely or causes it to move, except as otherwise provided in the Rules, the opponent incurs a penalty of one stroke. If the ball is moved, it must be replaced.

- *Ball at Rest Moved*
- *Ball Moved in Measuring*
- *Wrong Ball*

Ball in Motion Deflected or Stopped (Rule 19–3)

- <u>No penalty</u>: If a player's ball is accidentally deflected or stopped by an opponent, his caddie or his equipment, there is no penalty.

  OPTION A—<u>Play another stroke</u>: The player may, before another stroke is made by either side, cancel the stroke and play a ball without penalty as nearly as possible at the spot from which the original ball was last played (see Rule *Making Next Stroke from Where Previous Stroke Made*).

  OPTION B—<u>Play it as it lies</u>: He may play the ball as it lies. However, if the player elects not to cancel the stroke and the ball has come to rest in or on the opponent's or his caddie's clothes or equipment, the player must through the green or in a hazard drop the ball, or on the putting green place the ball, as near as possible to where the article was when the ball came to rest in or on it.

- *Ball Striking Flagstick or Attendant*
- *Exerting Influence on Ball*

By Outside Agency

Ball at Rest Moved (Rule 18–1)

- <u>Ball replaced, no penalty</u>: If a ball at rest is moved by an outside agency, there is no penalty and the ball must be replaced.

Ball in Motion Deflected or Stopped (Rule 19–1)

- <u>Ball played as it lies</u>: If a ball in motion is accidentally deflected or stopped by any outside agency, it is a rub of the green, there is no penalty and the ball must be played as it lies.

   <u>EXCEPTION when ball rests on moving object</u>: If a ball in motion after a stroke other than on the putting green comes to rest in or on any moving or animate outside agency, the player must, through the green or in a hazard, drop the ball, or on the putting green place the ball, as near as possible to the spot where the outside agency was when the ball came to rest in or on it, and;

   <u>EXCEPTION on the putting green</u>: If a ball in motion after a stroke on the putting green is deflected or stopped by, or comes to rest in or on, any moving or animate outside agency except a worm or an insect, the stroke is canceled. The ball must be replaced and the stroke replayed.

- <u>Ball not recoverable</u>: If the ball is not immediately recoverable, another ball may be substituted.

- <u>Ball purposely deflected</u>: If the referee or the Committee determines that a player's ball has been purposely deflected or stopped by an outside agency, see Rule *Points Not Covered by Rules*. If the outside agency is a fellow–competitor or his caddie, Rule *Exerting Influence on Ball* applies to the fellow–competitor.

- *Ball at Rest Moved*

- *By Another Ball*
- *Outside Agency*

By Player, Partner, Caddie or Equipment

Ball at Rest Moved (Rule 18–2)

- <u>Penalty of one(1) stroke</u>: When a player's ball is *in play*, if:

  (i) the player, his partner or either of their caddies lifts or moves it, touches it purposely (except with a club in the act of addressing it) or causes it to move except as permitted by a Rule; or

  (ii) equipment of the player or his partner causes the ball to move, the player incurs a penalty of one stroke.

- <u>Ball replaced</u>: If the ball is moved, it must be replaced unless the movement of the ball occurs after the player has begun the stroke or the backward movement of the club for the stroke and the stroke is made.

- <u>No Penalty</u>: Under the Rules there is no penalty if a player accidentally causes his ball to move in the following circumstances:

  (a) In searching for a ball in a hazard covered by loose impediments or sand, for a ball in an abnormal ground condition or for a ball believed to be in water in a water hazard (See *Searching for Ball*);

  (b) In repairing a hole plug or ball mark (See *Repair of Hole Plugs*);

  (c) In measuring (See *Ball Moved in Measuring*);

  (d) In lifting a ball under a Rule (See *Lifting and Marking*);

  (e) In placing or replacing a ball under a Rule (See *By Whom and Where*);

(f) In removing a loose impediment on the putting green (See *Relief; Loose Impediments*);

(g) In removing movable obstructions (See *Movable Obstruction*)

- Ball Moving After Address: If a player's ball in play moves (see *Ball Moves*) after he has addressed it (other than as a result of a stroke), the player is deemed to have moved the ball and incurs a penalty of one stroke. The ball must be replaced unless the movement of the ball occurs after the player has begun the stroke or the backward movement of the club for the stroke and the stroke is made.

Ball in Motion Deflected or Stopped (Rule 19–2)

- Match Play: If a player's ball is accidentally deflected or stopped by himself, his partner or either of their caddies or equipment, he loses the hole.

- Stroke Play: If a competitor's ball is accidentally deflected or stopped by himself, his partner or either of their caddies or equipment, the competitor incurs a penalty of two strokes. The ball must be played as it lies, except when it comes to rest in or on the competitor's, his partner's or either of their caddies' clothes or equipment, in which case the competitor must through the green or in a hazard drop the ball, or on the putting green place the ball, as near as possible to where the article was when the ball came to rest in or on it.

- *Dropping and Re-Dropping*
- *Exerting Influence on Ball*

C

Caddie (Rule 6–4)

- <u>Definition</u>: A *caddie* is one who assists the player in accordance with the Rules, which may include carrying or handling the player's clubs during play. When one caddie is employed by more than one player, he is always deemed to be the caddie of the player whose ball is involved, and equipment carried by him is deemed to be that player's equipment, except when the caddie acts upon specific directions of another player, in which case he is considered to be that other player's caddie.

- <u>Caddie breaks a rule</u>: If a caddie breaks a rule, the player takes the penalty.

- <u>More than one caddie</u>: The player may be assisted by a caddie, but he is limited to only one caddie at any one time. A player having more than one caddie in breach of this Rule must immediately upon the discovery that a breach has occurred ensure that he has no more than one caddie at any one time during the remainder of the stipulated round. Otherwise, the player is DISQUALIFIED.

- <u>Prohibit caddies</u>: The Committee may prohibit the use of caddies or restrict a player in his choice of caddie.

- <u>Match Play</u>: At the conclusion of the hole at which the breach is discovered, the state of the match is adjusted by deducting one hole for each hole at which a breach occurred; maximum deduction per round—Two holes.

- <u>Stroke Play</u>: Two strokes for each hole at which any breach occurred; maximum penalty per round—Four strokes.

- <u>Match or Stroke Play</u>: In the event of a breach between the play of two holes, the penalty applies to the next hole.

- *Advice*
- *Clubs*
- *Best-Ball and Four-Ball Match Play*
- *Bogey and Par Competitions*
- *Four-Ball Stroke Play* (more than one; failure to correct breach)
- *Stableford Competitions*
- *The Player*
- *Three-Ball Match Play* (touches, moves, stops, deflects ball)

Calcuttas

- *Gambling*

Camps

- *Instruction*

Cancel

All scores
- *Committee*

The stroke
- *Order of Play—Match Play*
- *Playing from Outside Teeing Ground*

Card

- *Scoring and Scorecard*

Care of the Course

Etiquette
- *Bunkers*
- *Repair of Divots, Ball-Marks, and Damage by Shoes*
- *Preventing Unnecessary Damage*

Career

- *Use of Golf Skill or Reputation*

Carry and roll of the ball

- *The Ball*

Cart path

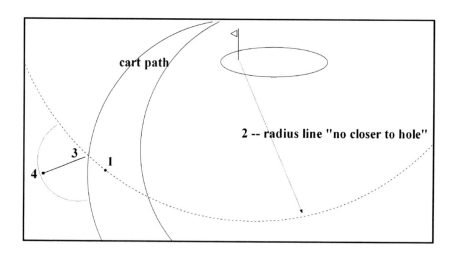

1—Ball comes to rest on cart path.

2—Establish radius line "no closer to hole."

3—Find ball location that provides nearest point of relief for stance and swing.

4—Drop zone is 1 club length from **3**, no closer to hole.

- *Immovable Obstruction*

Cash prizes

- *Gambling*

Casual Water

- <u>Definition</u>: *Casual water* is any temporary accumulation of water on the course, that is visible before or after the player takes his stance, and is not in a water hazard. A ball is in casual water when it lies in or any part of it touches the casual water.

- <u>Snow and natural ice</u>, other than frost, are either casual water or loose impediments, at the option of the player.

- <u>Manufactured ice</u> is an obstruction.

- <u>Dew and frost</u> are not casual water.

Celebrity

- *Expenses*

Championship positions (tee)

- *Course Record*

Change the Rules

- *Artificial Devices and Unusual Equipment*

Changed or adjustment of clubs

- *Playing Characteristics Changed*

Changing ball's playing characteristics

- *Foreign Material*

Characteristics

Ball
- *Foreign Material*

Club
- *Playing Characteristics Changed*

Charity

- *Expenses*

Check

Addition
- *Committee*

Score
- *Stroke Play*

Check your stroke

- <u>Does not count</u>: If you check your clubhead before it reaches the ball, then it is NOT A STROKE and you do not have to score it.

- *Miss the ball*

Chipping

- *Practice*

Choice of caddie

- *Caddie*

Circular grip

- *Grip*

Claims

- <u>Match Play</u>: If there is a claim and no one of authority is available to resolve the matter, go on with the match. Once any player tees off from the next tee, or after all the players have left the putting green of the last hole, the claim expires.

- *Disputes and Decisions*
- *Doubt as to Procedure, Disputes and Claims*

Cleaning Ball (Rule 21)

- <u>Ball may be cleaned</u>: A ball on the putting green may be cleaned when lifted under Rule *Lifting and Cleaning Ball.*

Exceptions

a. To determine if it is unfit for play (Rule *Ball Unfit for Play*);

b. For identification (Rule *Identifying Ball*), in which case it may be cleaned only to the extent necessary for identification; or

c. Because it is assisting or interfering with play (Rule *Searching for and Identifying Ball*).

Penalties

- <u>During play of a hole</u>: If a player cleans his ball during play of a hole except as provided in this Rule, he incurs a penalty of one stroke and the ball, if lifted, must be replaced.

- <u>Fails to replace ball</u>: If a player who is required to replace a ball fails to do so, he incurs the penalty for breach of Rule *Placing and Replacing*, but there is no additional penalty under this Rule.

- <u>No additional penalty</u>: If a player incurs a penalty for failing to act in accordance with Rule *Ball Unfit for Play*, *Identifying Ball*, or *Ball Assisting or Interfering with Play*, there is no additional penalty under this Rule.

- *Movable Obstruction*

Closed competition

- *Disputes and Decisions*

Closely mown area

- *Embedded Ball*

Cloth

- *Artificial Devices and Unusual Equipment*

Club characteristics

- *Playing Characteristics Changed*

Club Face

- General: The material and construction of, or any treatment to, the face or clubhead must not have the effect at impact of a spring, or impart significantly more or less spin to the ball than a standard steel face, or have any other effect which would unduly influence the movement of the ball. The face of the club must be hard and rigid (some exceptions may be made for putters) and, except for such markings listed below, must be smooth and must not have any degree of concavity.

- Impact Area Roughness and Material: Except for markings specified in the following paragraphs, the surface roughness within the area where impact is intended (the "impact area") must not exceed that of decorative sandblasting, or of fine milling. The whole of the impact area must be of the same material. Exceptions may be made for wooden clubs.

- Impact Area Markings: Markings in the impact area must not have sharp edges or raised lips as determined by a finger test. Grooves or punch marks in the impact area must meet the following specifications:

  (i) Grooves: A series of straight grooves with diverging sides and a symmetrical cross-section may be used.

  (a) The width and cross-section must be consistent across the face of the club and along the length of the grooves.

(b) Any rounding of groove edges shall be in the form of a radius which does not exceed 0.020 inches (0.508 mm).

(c) The width of the grooves must not exceed 0.035 inches (0.9 mm), using the 30 degree method of measurement on file with the United States Golf Association.

(d) The distance between edges of adjacent grooves must not be less than three times the width of a groove, and not less than 0.075 inches (1.905 mm).

(e) The depth of a groove must not exceed 0.020 inches (0.508 mm). Exception: *Club Face Markings*.

(ii) <u>Punch Marks</u>: Punch marks may be used.

(a) The area of any such mark must not exceed 0.0044 square inches (2.84 sq. mm).

(b) A mark must not be closer to an adjacent mark than 0.168 inches (4.27 mm) measured from center to center.

(c) The depth of a punch mark must not exceed 0.040 inches (1.02 mm).

(d) If punch marks are used in combination with grooves, a punch mark must not be closer to a groove than 0.168 inches (4.27 mm), measured from center to center.

- <u>Decorative Markings</u>: The center of the impact area may be indicated by a design within the boundary of a square whose sides are 0.375 inches (9.53 mm) in length. Such a design must not unduly influence the movement of the ball. Decorative markings are permitted outside the impact area.

- <u>Non-metallic Club Face Markings</u>: The above specifications apply to clubs on which the impact area of the face is of metal or a material of similar hardness. They do not apply to clubs with faces made of other materials and whose loft angle is 24 degrees or less, but markings which could unduly influence the movement of the ball are prohibited. Clubs with this type of face and a loft angle exceeding 24 degrees may have grooves of maximum width 0.040 inches (1.02 mm) and maximum depth 1 1/2 times the groove width, but must otherwise conform to the markings specifications above.

- <u>Putter Face Markings</u>: The specifications above with regard to roughness, material and markings in the impact area do not apply to putters.

- *Design*
- *Foreign Material*

Club grip

- *Artificial Devices and Unusual Equipment*

Club is damaged

- *Damaged Clubs*

Club may be grounded only lightly

- *Improving Lie, Area of Intended Stance or Swing, or Line of Play*

Club's lie and loft

- *Damaged Clubs*

Clubhead

Plain in Shape

- <u>Not permitted</u>: The clubhead must be generally plain in shape. All parts must be rigid, structural in nature and functional. It is not practicable to define plain in shape precisely and comprehensively but features which are deemed to be in breach of this requirement and are therefore not permitted include:

(i) holes: holes through the head,

(ii) transparent material: transparent material added for other than decorative or structural purposes,

(iii) appendages: appendages to the main body of the head such as knobs, plates, rods or fins, for the purpose of meeting dimensional specifications, for aiming or for any other purpose. Exceptions may be made for putters. Any furrows in or runners on the sole must not extend into the face.

Dimensions and Size

- Woods: When the club is in a 60 degree lie angle, the dimensions of the clubhead must be such that:

    (a) the distance from the heel to the toe of the clubhead is greater than the distance from the face to the back;

    (b) the distance from the heel to the toe of the clubhead is not greater than 5 inches (127 mm); and

    (c) the distance from the sole to the crown of the clubhead is not greater than 2.8 inches (71.12 mm).

    Dimensions are measured: These dimensions are measured on horizontal lines between vertical projections of the outermost points of:

    - the heel and the toe; and

    - the face and the back; and on vertical lines between the horizontal projections of the outermost points of the sole and the crown. If the outermost point of the heel is not clearly defined, it is deemed to be 0.875 inches (22.23 mm) above the horizontal plane on which the club is lying.

<u>Size</u>: The size of the clubhead must not exceed 28.06 cubic inches (460 cubic centimeters), plus a tolerance of 0.61 cubic inches (10 cubic centimeters).

- <u>Irons and Putters</u>: When the clubhead is in its normal address position, the dimensions of the head must be such that the distance from the heel to the toe is greater than the distance from the face to the back. For traditionally shaped heads, these dimensions will be measured on horizontal lines between vertical projections of the outermost points of:
  - the heel and toe; and
  - the face and back.
  - for unusually shaped heads, the toe to heel dimension may be made at the face.

Striking Faces

- <u>One striking face</u>: The clubhead must have only one striking face, except that a putter may have two such faces if their characteristics are the same, and they are opposite each other.

- *Club Face*
- *Damaged Clubs* (becomes loose)
- *Design*

Clubs (Rule 4)

Rules of play

- <u>Single unit</u>: Must be a single unit that is not detachable or adjustable.

- <u>14 clubs</u>: Only 14 clubs in the bag. You can start with fewer, and then add clubs to make a complete set of 14.

- <u>Cannot change</u>: Once you select them, you cannot change them.

- <u>Replace but not borrow</u>: If a club becomes broken or unfit for play, you may replace it, but you cannot borrow a club.

- <u>Too many clubs</u>: Once you discover you're carrying too many clubs, you must immediately announce that you're taking the extra club(s) out of play and not use it again. If you fail to do this you can be DISQUALIFIED.

- <u>Match Play</u>: You can share clubs with your partner.

- <u>Penalty for Breach of Rule</u>: *Match play*, Lose one hole for every hole in error, but a maximum of two holes; *Stroke play*, two strokes per hole in error, but a maximum of four strokes.

- *Best-Ball and Four-Ball Match Play*
- *Bogey and Par Competitions*
- *Caddie*
- *Damaged Clubs*
- *Form and Make of Clubs*
- *Four-Ball Stroke Play*
- *Maximum of 14 Clubs*
- *Playing Characteristics Changed*
- *Stableford Competitions*

General specifications

- <u>Definition</u>: A club is an implement designed to be used for striking the ball and generally comes in three forms: woods, irons and putters distinguished by shape and intended use.

- <u>Putter</u>: A putter is a club with a loft not exceeding ten degrees designed primarily for use on the putting green.

- <u>Composition</u>: The club must not be substantially different from the traditional and customary form and make. The club must be composed of a shaft and a head. All parts of the club must be fixed so that the club is one unit, and it must have no external attachments except as otherwise permitted by the Rules.

Adjustability

- Permitted adjustments: Woods and irons must not be designed to be adjustable except for weight. Putters may be designed to be adjustable for weight and some other forms of adjustability are also permitted. All methods of adjustment permitted by the Rules require that:

   (i) readily made: the adjustment cannot be readily made;

   (ii) adjustable parts fixed: all adjustable parts are firmly fixed and there is no reasonable likelihood of them working loose during a round; and

   (iii) conformity: all configurations of adjustment conform with the Rules. The disqualification penalty for purposely changing the playing characteristics of a club during a stipulated round (Rule *Playing Characteristics Changed*) applies to all clubs including a putter.

Length

- Minimum and maximum: The overall length of the club must be at least 18 inches (457.2 mm) and, except for putters, must not exceed 48 inches (1,219.2 mm). For woods and irons, the measurement of length is taken when the club is lying on a horizontal plane and the sole is set against a 60 degree plane. The length is defined as the distance from the point of the intersection between the two planes to the top of the grip. For putters, the measurement of length is taken from the top of the grip along the axis of the shaft or a straight line extension of it to the sole of the club.

Alignment

- Shaft axis: When the club is in its normal address position the shaft must be so aligned that:

(i) <u>axis perpendicular to line of play</u>: the projection of the straight part of the shaft on to the vertical plane through the toe and heel must diverge from the vertical by at least 10 degrees;

(ii) <u>axis along line of play</u>: the projection of the straight part of the shaft on to the vertical plane along the intended line of play must not diverge from the vertical by more than 20 degrees forward or 10 degrees backward.

- <u>Heel of club</u>: Except for putters, all of the heel portion of the club must lie within 0.625 inches (15.88 mm) of the plane containing the axis of the straight part of the shaft and the intended (horizontal) line of play.

- *Design*

Colleges

- *Instruction*

Combine stroke and match play

- *Committee*

Commentary

- *Use of Golf Skill or Reputation*

Commercial purposes

- *Professionalism*

Committee (Rule 33)

- <u>Definition</u>: The *Committee* is the committee in charge of the competition or, if the matter does not arise in a competition, the committee in charge of the course.

- *Discontinuance of Play; Resumption of Play*
- *Procedure When Play Suspended by Committee*
- *Scoring and Scorecard*

Conditions; Waiving Rule (Rule 33–1)

- <u>Conditions</u>: The Committee must establish the conditions under which a competition is to be played.

- <u>No power to waive rule</u>: The Committee has no power to waive a Rule of Golf.

- <u>Stroke and match play cannot be combined</u>: Certain specific Rules governing stroke play are so substantially different from those governing match play that combining the two forms of play is not practicable and is not permitted. The results of matches played and the scores returned in these circumstances must not be accepted.

- <u>Referee's duties</u>: In stroke play the Committee may limit a referee's duties.

The Course (Rule 33–2)

- <u>Defining Bounds and Margins</u>: The Committee must define accurately:

  (i) the course and out of bounds,
  (ii) the margins of water hazards and lateral water hazards,
  (iii) ground under repair, and
  (iv) obstructions and integral parts of the course.

- <u>New Holes</u>: New holes should be made on the day on which a stroke play competition begins and at such other times as the

Committee considers necessary, provided all competitors in a single round play with each hole cut in the same position. <u>Damaged hole</u>: When it is impossible for a damaged hole to be repaired so that it conforms with the Definition, the Committee may make a new hole in a nearby similar position. <u>Round played on more than one day</u>: Where a single round is to be played on more than one day, the Committee may provide in the conditions of a competition that the holes and teeing grounds may be differently situated on each day of the competition, provided that, on any one day, all competitors play with each hole and each teeing ground in the same position.

- <u>Practice Ground</u>: Where there is no practice ground available outside the area of a competition course, the Committee should establish the area on which players may practice on any day of a competition, if it is practicable to do so. On any day of a stroke play competition, the Committee should not normally permit practice on or to a putting green or from a hazard of the competition course.

- <u>Course Unplayable</u>: If the Committee or its authorized representative considers that for any reason the course is not in a playable condition or that there are circumstances that render the proper playing of the game impossible, it may, in match play or stroke play, order a temporary suspension of play or, in stroke play, declare play null and void and cancel all scores for the round in question. When a round is canceled, all penalties incurred in that round are canceled (see Rule *Discontinuance of Play; Resumption of Play*).

Times of Starting and Groups (Rule 33–3)

- <u>Times and groups</u>: The Committee must establish the times of starting and, in stroke play, arrange the groups in which competitors must play.

- <u>Match play time limit</u>: When a match–play competition is played over an extended period, the Committee establishes the limit of time within which each round must be completed. When players are allowed to arrange the date of their match within these limits, the Committee should announce that the match must be played at a stated time on the last day of the period unless the players agree to a prior date.

Handicap Stroke Table (Rule 33–4)

- <u>Order of handicap holes</u>: The Committee must publish a table indicating the order of holes at which handicap strokes are to be given or received.

Scorecard (Rule 33–5)

- <u>Provide Scorecards</u>: In stroke play, the Committee must provide each competitor with a Scorecard containing the date and the competitor's name or, in foursomes or four–ball stroke play, the competitors' names.

- <u>Check addition, apply handicap</u>: In stroke play, the Committee is responsible for the addition of scores and the application of the handicap recorded on the Scorecard.

- <u>Four-ball stroke play</u>: In four–ball stroke play, the Committee is responsible for recording the better–ball score for each hole and in the process applying the handicaps recorded on the Scorecard, and adding the better–ball scores.

- <u>Bogey, par and Stableford</u>: In bogey, par and Stableford competitions, the Committee is responsible for applying the handicap recorded on the Scorecard and determining the result of each hole and the overall result or points total.

- <u>Competitor record name</u>: The Committee may request that each competitor record the date and his name on his Scorecard.

Decision of Ties (Rule 33–6)

- <u>Announce decision</u>: The Committee must announce the manner, day and time for the decision of a halved match or of a tie, whether played on level terms or under handicap. A halved match must not be decided by stroke play. A tie in stroke play must not be decided by a match.

Disqualification Penalty; Committee Discretion (Rule 33–7)

- Discretion: A penalty of disqualification may in exceptional individual cases be waived, modified or imposed if the Committee considers such action warranted. Any penalty less than disqualification must not be waived or modified.

- Serious breach of etiquette: If a Committee considers that a player is guilty of a serious breach of etiquette, it may impose a penalty of disqualification under this Rule.

Local Rules (Rule 33–8)

- Policy: The Committee may establish Local Rules for local abnormal conditions if they are consistent with the policy set forth in *Local Rules*.

- Waiving or Modifying a Rule: A Rule of Golf must not be waived by a Local Rule. However, if a Committee considers that local abnormal conditions interfere with the proper playing of the game to the extent that it is necessary to make a Local Rule that modifies the Rules of Golf, the Local Rule must be authorized by the USGA.

- *Disputes and Decisions*
- *Procedure for Enforcement of the Rules*
- *Reinstatement of Amateur Status*

Committee Decision

- Decision is final: The Committee's decision is final, subject to an Appeal as provided in *Procedure for Enforcement of the Rules* and *Reinstatement of Amateur Status*.

- *Amateur Status*
- *Disputes and Decisions*
- *Reinstatement of Amateur Status* (sole authority)

Compensation

- *Instruction*
- *Use of Golf Skill or Reputation*

Competitions

- *Amateurism*
- *Committee*
- *Course Record*
- *Disputes and Decisions* (competition has closed)
- *Use of Golf Skill or Reputation*

Types
- *Bogey and Par Competitions*
- *Stableford Competitions*

Competitor

- <u>Definition</u>: A *competitor* is a player in a stroke play competition. A *fellow-competitor* is any person with whom the competitor plays. Neither is partner of the other. In stroke play foursome and four–ball competitions, where the context so admits, the word *competitor* or *fellow-competitor* includes his partner.

- *Refusal to Comply with a Rule* (stroke play)
- *Second ball*

Competitor's name

- *Committee*

Complete the hole with two balls

- *Doubt as to Procedure* (stroke play)

Comply with a Rule

- *Refusal to Comply with a Rule* (stroke play)

Compulsory sweepstakes

- *Gambling*

Concavity

- *Club Face*
- *Grip*

Concession of Next Stroke, Hole or Match
(Rule 2–4)

- <u>Concede a stroke</u>: A player may concede his opponent's next stroke at any time provided the opponent's ball is at rest. The opponent is considered to have holed out with his next stroke and the ball may be removed by either side.

- <u>Concede a hole</u>: A player may concede a hole at any time prior to the start or conclusion of that hole.

- <u>Concede a match</u>: A player may concede a match at any time prior to the start or conclusion of that match.

- <u>No decline or withdraw</u>: A concession may not be declined or withdrawn.

- *Ball Overhanging Hole*
- *Match Play*

Conditions

- *Abnormal Ground Conditions*
- *Artificial Devices and Unusual Equipment* (conditions that affect play)
- *Committee*
- *Use of Golf Skill or Reputation*

Conduct

- *Amateurism*
- *Other Conduct Incompatible with Amateurism*

Conform to requirements (ball)

- *Ball*

Conforming to Rules

- *Disputes and Decisions*

Confused

- <u>Play second ball</u>: If during stroke play you get confused about what you're allowed or supposed to do in a certain situation, you're allowed to play a second ball after telling the other players what you're going to do and which ball you will score for that hole. You must tell the Committee what happened before turning in your Scorecard, or you will be DISQUALIFIED. If what you decided to do after you were confused turned out to be the legal course to take, then the second ball will be your score.

Consideration for Other Players

Etiquette
- *No Disturbance or Distraction*
- *On the Putting Green*
- *Scoring*

Construction

- *Club Face*

Continue play

Hole
- *Procedure When Play Suspended by Committee*

Original ball
- *Provisional Ball*

Convert a prize into money

- *Prizes*

Correcting

- *Doubt as to Procedure* (stroke play)
- *Information as to Strokes Taken*
- *Playing from Outside Teeing Ground*
- *Stroke Play*
- *Threesomes and Foursomes* (correcting the error)
- *Wrong information*

Correctness of the decision given

- *Disputes and Decisions*

Counselor at a camp

- *Instruction*

Course

- <u>Definition</u>: The *course* is the whole area within any boundaries established by the Committee (see Rule *The Course*).

- *Committee* (course unplayable)

Course Record (Misc./1)

- <u>Made in competition</u>: The term *course record* is not defined in the Rules of Golf. However, it is generally accepted that a record score should be recognized as the official *course record* only if made in an individual stroke play competition (excluding bogey, par or Stableford competitions) with the holes and tee–markers in their proper medal or championship positions. It is recommended that a record score should not be recognized as the official *course record* if a Local Rule permitting preferred lies is in operation.

Covered ball

- *Searching for Ball*

Cracked ball

- *Ball Unfit for Play*

Creating or eliminating irregularities of surface

- *Improving Lie, Area of Intended Stance or Swing, or Line of Play*
- *Stance*

Cross-section

- *Club Face*
- *Grip*

Crown

- *Clubhead*

Customer

- *Expenses*

Cut ball

- *Ball Unfit for Play*

Cut holes

- *Committee*

D

Damage to putting green

- *Repair of Hole Plugs, Ball Marks, and Other Damage*

Damaged ball

- *Ball Unfit for Play*

Damaged Clubs: Repair and Replacement
(Rule 4–3)

- <u>Definition</u>: A club is *Unfit for Play* if it is substantially damaged, e.g., the shaft is dented, significantly bent or broken into pieces; the clubhead becomes loose, detached or significantly deformed; or the grip becomes loose. A club is not *Unfit for Play* solely because the club's lie or loft has been altered, or the clubhead is scratched.

- <u>During a round</u>: If, during a stipulated round, a player's club is damaged in the normal course of play, he may:

  (i) <u>Use the club</u>: use the club in its damaged state for the remainder of the stipulated round; or

  (ii) <u>Repair it</u>: without unduly delaying play, repair it or have it repaired; or

  (iii) <u>Replace it</u>: as an additional option available only if the club is unfit for play, replace the damaged club with any club.

- <u>Club out of play</u>: If, during a stipulated round, a player's club is damaged other than in the normal course of play rendering it

83

non–conforming or changing its playing characteristics, the club must not subsequently be used or replaced during the round.

- <u>Club damaged prior to round</u>: A player may use a club damaged prior to a round provided the club, in its damaged state, conforms with the Rules. Damage to a club that occurred prior to a round may be repaired during the round, provided the playing characteristics are not changed and play is not unduly delayed.

- <u>No delay</u>: The replacement of a club must not unduly delay play.

- <u>No borrowing</u>: The replacement of a club must not be made by borrowing any club selected for play by any other person playing on the course.

- <u>Penalty for Breach of Rule</u>: DISQUALIFICATION.

- *Best-Ball and Four-Ball Match Play*
- *Clubs*
- *Four-Ball Stroke Play*

Damaged hole

- *Committee*

Danger from lightning and other situations

- *Discontinuance of Play; Resumption of Play*
- *Procedure When Play Suspended by Committee*

Date of match

- *Committee*

Date of the person's last breach of the Rules

- *Reinstatement of Amateur Status*

Day after

- *Procedure When Play Resumed*

Debris

- *Ground Under Repair*
- *Loose Impediments*

Decisions

- *Committee* (ties)
- *Committee Decision* (is final)
- *Disputes and Decisions*
- *Procedure for Enforcement of the Rules* (Amateur Status)

Declared a handicap

- *Handicap*

Declining a concession

- *Concession of Next Stroke, Hole or Match*

Decorative features

- *Club Face* (markings and sandblasting)
- *Clubhead*

Define boundaries and margins

- *Committee*

Deflected or Stopped (ball)

- *By Another Ball*
- *By Opponent, Caddie or Equipment in Match Play*
- *By Outside Agency*
- *By Player, Partner, Caddie or Equipment*

Deformed club

- *Damaged Clubs*

Degree lie angle

- *Clubhead*

Delay of Play

- *Maximum of 14 Clubs*
- *Slow Play*
- *Undue Delay*

Deny reinstatement

- *Reinstatement of Amateur Status*

Depth of a groove or punch mark

- *Club Face*

Design

Ball
- *The Ball* (Appendix III)

Clubs (Appendix II)
- <u>Conformity</u>: A player in doubt as to the conformity of a club should consult the United States Golf Association (USGA).

- *Club Face*
- *Clubhead*
- *Clubs*
- *Grip*
- *Shaft*

Detachable

- *Clubs*

Detached club

- *Damaged Clubs*

Detrimental to Amateurism

- *Other Conduct Incompatible with Amateurism*

Devices

- *Artificial Devices and Unusual Equipment*

Dew and frost

- <u>Not casual water</u>: Dew and frost are NOT casual water.

- <u>Not loose impediments</u>: Dew and frost are NOT loose impediments.

- *Improving Lie, Area of Intended Stance or Swing, or Line of Play*

Diameter

- *The Ball*

Different holes and teeing grounds

- *Committee*

Difficult lie

- *Ball Played as it Lies*

Dimensional specifications (club)

- *Clubhead*

Discolored ball

- *Ball Unfit for Play*

Discontinuance of Play; Resumption of Play
(Rule 6–8a)

- <u>Permitted reasons for discontinuance</u>: The player must not discontinue play unless:

(i) <u>Committee</u>: the Committee has suspended play; or, he is seeking a decision from the Committee on a doubtful or disputed point.

(ii) <u>Weather</u>: he believes there is danger from lightning; bad weather is not of itself a good reason for discontinuing play.

(iii) <u>Illness</u>: there is some other good reason such as sudden illness.

- <u>Disqualification</u>: If the player discontinues play without specific permission from the Committee, he must report to the Committee as soon as practicable. If he does so and the Committee considers his reason satisfactory, there is no penalty. Otherwise, the player is DISQUALIFIED.

- <u>Match Play</u>: Players discontinuing match play by agreement are not subject to disqualification unless by so doing the competition is delayed. Leaving the course does not of itself constitute discontinuance of play.

- *Best-Ball and Four-Ball Match Play*
- *Bogey and Par Competitions*
- *Committee*
- *Four-Ball Stroke Play*
- *Lifting Ball When Play Discontinued*
- *Procedure When Play Resumed*
- *Procedure When Play Suspended by Committee*
- *Stableford Competitions*
- *The Player*

Discretion of Committee

- *Committee*

Disputes and Decisions (Rule 34)

Claims and Penalties (Rule 34–1)

- Match Play: If there is a dispute and no one of authority is available to resolve the matter, go on with the match. Once any player tees off from the next tee, or after all the players have left the putting green of the last hole, the dispute expires. If a claim is lodged with the Committee under Rule *Doubt as to Procedure; Disputes and Claims*, a decision should be given as soon as possible so that the state of the match may, if necessary, be adjusted. If a claim is not made in accordance with Rule *Doubt as to Procedure; Disputes and Claims*, it must not be considered by the Committee. There is no time limit on applying the disqualification penalty for a breach of Rule *Agreement to Waive Rules*.

- Stroke Play: In stroke play, a penalty must not be rescinded, modified or imposed after the competition has closed. A competition is closed when the result has been officially announced or, in stroke–play qualifying followed by match play, when the player has teed off in his first match.

   Exceptions: A penalty of disqualification must be imposed after the competition has closed if a competitor:

   (i) was in breach of Rule *Agreement to Waive Rules*; or

   (ii) returned a Scorecard on which he had recorded a handicap that, before the competition closed, he knew was higher than that to which he was entitled, and this affected the number of strokes received (Rule *Handicap—Stroke play*); or

   (iii) returned a score for any hole lower than actually taken (Rule *Stroke Play—Wrong Score for Hole*) for any reason other than failure to include a penalty that, before the competition closed, he did not know he had incurred; or

   (iv) knew, before the competition closed, that he had been in breach of any other Rule for which the penalty is disqualification.

Referee's Decision (Rule 34–2)

- <u>Decision is final</u>: If a referee has been appointed by the Committee, his decision is final.

Committee's Decision (Rule 34–3)

- <u>No referee</u>: In the absence of a referee, any dispute or doubtful point on the Rules must be referred to the Committee, whose decision is final.

- <u>Committee may refer to USGA</u>: If the Committee cannot come to a decision, it may refer the dispute or doubtful point to the Rules of Golf Committee of the United States Golf Association, whose decision is final.

- <u>Player(s) may appeal to USGA</u>: If the dispute or doubtful point has not been referred to the Rules of Golf Committee, the player or players may request that an agreed statement be referred through a duly authorized representative of the Committee to the Rules of Golf Committee for an opinion as to the correctness of the decision given. The reply will be sent to this authorized representative.

- <u>Play not conforming to Rules</u>: If play is conducted other than in accordance with the Rules of Golf, the Rules of Golf Committee will not give a decision on any question.

- *Ball Unfit for Play*
- *Discontinuance of Play; Resumption of Play*
- *Doubt as to Procedure; Disputes and Claims*

Disqualification

- <u>Ignore rules</u>: If players willingly ignore the rules of play.

- <u>Extra clubs</u>: If you fail to immediately announce that you're taking the extra club(s) out of play and not use it again (see *Clubs*).

- <u>Illegal ball</u>: Using an illegal ball (see *Ball*).

- <u>Wrong handicap</u>: If a player gives too high a handicap **and** it affects his score in a handicap competition.

- <u>More than one caddie</u>: If a player uses more than one caddie (see *Caddie*).

- <u>Incorrect score</u>: If a player incorrectly scores any hole on his card, signs the card, and turns in the card (see *Scoring and Scorecard*).

- <u>Undue delay</u>: If a player causes repeated *undue delay*.

Stroke Play

- <u>Confused</u>: If during stroke play you get confused about what you're allowed or supposed to do in a certain situation, you're allowed to play a second ball after telling the other players what you're going to do and which ball you will score for that hole. You must tell the Committee what happened before turning in your Scorecard, or you will be DISQUALIFIED.

- <u>Fail to hole out</u>: If you fail to hole out on any hole.

- <u>Incorrect score</u>: If you record a lower score than you should have.

- <u>Practice</u>: If you practice when you shouldn't.

- *Agreement to Waive Rules*
- *Artificial Devices and Unusual Equipment*
- *Ball*
- *Best-Ball and Four-Ball Match Play*
- *Clubs*
- *Committee*
- *Discontinuance of Play (Resumption of Play)*
- *Failure to Hole Out*
- *Handicap Competition*
- *Playing out of turn*
- *Practice*

- *Scoring and Scorecard*
- *Second ball*
- *Undue delay*
- *Refusal to Comply with a Rule* (stroke play)

Disregard

Penalty
- *Provisional Ball*

Strokes
- *Playing from Wrong Place*

Distance

- *Artificial Devices and Unusual Equipment* (used to measure)
- *Clubhead* (specifications)
- *The Ball* (specifications)

Divots

- <u>Replace all divots</u>: Replace all divots in the fairway.

- *Improving Lie, Area of Intended Stance or Swing, or Line of Play*

Dog

- *Burrowing Animal*

Donors

- *Prizes*

Dormie

- <u>Definition</u>: A side is *dormie* when it is as many holes up as there are left to play.

- *Match Play*

Doubt as to Procedure; Disputes and Claims

Stroke Play (Rule 3–3)

- <u>Complete hole with two balls</u>: In stroke play, if a competitor is doubtful of his rights or the correct procedure during the play of a hole he may, without penalty, complete the hole with two balls. After the doubtful situation has arisen and before taking further action, the competitor must announce to his marker or a fellow–competitor that he intends to play two balls and which ball he wishes to count if the Rules permit.

- <u>Report to Committee</u>: The competitor must report the facts of the situation to the Committee before returning his Scorecard. If he fails to do so, he is DISQUALIFIED.

- <u>Select which ball to count</u>: If the ball that the competitor selected in advance to count has been played in accordance with the Rules, the score with that ball is the competitor's score for the hole. Otherwise, the score with the other ball counts if the Rules allow the procedure adopted for that ball.

- <u>Failure to announce which ball to count</u>: If the competitor fails to announce in advance his decision to complete the hole with two balls, or which ball he wishes to count, the score with the original ball counts, provided it has been played in accordance with the Rules. If the original ball is not one of the balls being played, the first ball put into play counts, provided it has been played in accordance with the Rules. Otherwise, the score with the other ball counts if the Rules allow the procedure adopted for that ball.

Match Play (Rule 2–5)

- <u>Player may make a claim</u>: In match play, if a doubt or dispute arises between the players, a player may make a claim. If no duly authorized representative of the Committee is available within a reasonable time, the players must continue the match without delay.

- <u>Claim made before playing next hole</u>: The Committee may consider a claim only if the player making the claim notifies his opponent (i) that he is making a claim, (ii) of the facts of the situation and (iii) that he wants a ruling. The claim must be made before any player in the match plays from the next teeing ground or, in the case of the last hole of the match, before all players in the match leave the putting green.

- <u>Claim made after hole or match</u>: A later claim may not be considered by the Committee unless it is based on facts previously unknown to the player making the claim and he had been given wrong information by an opponent. Once the result of the match has been officially announced, a later claim may not be considered by the Committee unless it is satisfied that the opponent knew he was giving wrong information.

- *Amateurism* (rules and appeal process)
- *Discontinuance of Play; Resumption of Play*
- *Disputes and Decisions*
- *Match Play*
- *Stroke Play*

Dried up water hazard

- A dried–up water hazard is STILL a water hazard.

Dropping and Re-Dropping (Rule 20–2)

- <u>By Whom and How</u>: A ball to be dropped under the Rules must be dropped by the player himself. He must stand erect, hold the ball at shoulder height and arm's length and drop it. If a ball is dropped by any other person or in any other manner and the error is not corrected as provided in Rule *Lifting Ball Incorrectly Substituted, Dropped or Placed*, the player incurs a penalty of one stroke.

• <u>Ball touches something during drop</u>: If the ball touches the player, his partner, either of their caddies or their equipment before or after it strikes a part of the course, the ball must be re–dropped, without penalty (except, see Rule *Exerting Influence on Ball*). There is no limit to the number of times a ball must be re–dropped in these circumstances.

• <u>Where to Drop</u>: When a ball is to be dropped as near as possible to a specific spot, it must be dropped not nearer the hole than the specific spot which, if it is not precisely known to the player, must be estimated.

• <u>Must first strike the course</u>: A ball when dropped must first strike a part of the course where the applicable Rule requires it to be dropped. If it is not so dropped, Rules *Lifting Ball Incorrectly Substituted, Dropped or Placed* and *Playing from Wrong Place* apply.

• <u>When to Re-Drop</u>: A dropped ball must be re–dropped without penalty if it:

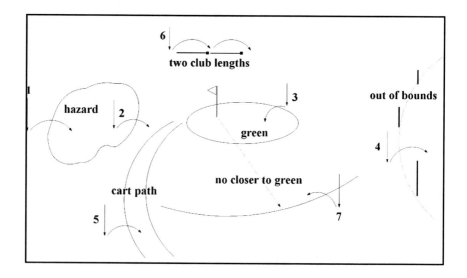

1—rolls into and comes to rest in a hazard;

2—rolls out of and comes to rest outside a hazard;

3—rolls onto and comes to rest on a putting green;

4—rolls and comes to rest out of bounds;

5—rolls to and comes to rest in a position where there is interference by the condition from which relief was taken under Rule *Immovable Obstruction*, Rule *Abnormal Ground Conditions*, Rule *Wrong Putting Green*, or a *Local Rule*, or rolls back into the pitchmark from which it was lifted under Rule *Embedded Ball*;

6—rolls and comes to rest more than two club-lengths from where it first struck a part of the course; or

7—rolls and comes to rest nearer the hole than: (a) its original position or estimated position (see *Where to Drop* above) unless otherwise permitted by the Rules; or (b) the nearest point of relief or maximum available relief (Rule *Immovable Obstruction*, *Abnormal Ground Conditions* or *Wrong Putting Green*); or (c) the point where the original ball last crossed the margin of the water hazard or lateral water hazard (Rule *Relief for Ball in Water Hazard*).

- Placed near where first struck course: If the ball when re–dropped rolls into any position listed above, it must be placed as near as possible to the spot where it first struck a part of the course when re–dropped.

- Ball not recoverable: If a ball to be re–dropped or placed under this Rule is not immediately recoverable, another ball may be substituted.

- Ball moves after drop: If a ball when dropped or re–dropped comes to rest and subsequently moves, the ball must be played as it lies, unless the provisions of any other Rule apply.

- *Ball Lost in Obstruction*
- *Ball Played Within Water Hazard*
- *Ball Unplayable*
- *Improving Lie, Swing, or Line of Play*
- *Lifting the Ball, Dropping, and Placing*
- *Relief for Ball in Water Hazard*
- *When Ball Dropped or Placed is in Play*
- *Wrong Putting Green*

Drying agents

- *Artificial Devices and Unusual Equipment*

During......

- <u>Play of Hole</u>: *Best-Ball and Four-Ball Match Play; Order of Play— Stroke Play*

- <u>Round</u>: *Practice During Round*

- <u>Search</u>: *By Opponent, Caddie or Equipment in Match Play*

Duties of referee

- *Committee*

E

Edges of adjacent grooves

- *Club Face*

Educational institution

- *Expenses*

Effect at impact

- *Club Face*

Effect of Other Penalties

- *Best-Ball and Four-Ball Match Play*
- *Four-Ball Stroke Play*

Eligibility

- *Amateurism*

Eliminating irregularities of surface

- *Improving Lie, Area of Intended Stance or Swing, or Line of Play*

Embedded Ball (Rule 25–2)

- <u>Lift, clean and drop</u>: A ball embedded in its own pitch–mark in the ground in any closely mown area through the green may be lifted, cleaned and dropped, without penalty, as near as possible to the spot where it lay but not nearer the hole.

- <u>Closely mown area</u>: The ball when dropped must first strike a part of the course through the green. *Closely mown area* means any area of the course, including paths through the rough, cut to fairway height or less.

- *Abnormal Ground Conditions*
- *Dropping and Re-Dropping*

Employee of an educational institution or system

- *Instruction*

Endanger amateur status

- *Gambling*

Enforcement of the Rules

- *Procedure for Enforcement of the Rules*

Entering

Professional qualifier; agreement with agent
- *Professionalism*

Equidistant from the hole

- *Order of Play—Match Play*

Equipment

- <u>Definition</u>: *Equipment* is anything used, worn or carried by or for the player except any ball he has played at the hole being played and any small object, such as a coin or a tee, when used to mark the position of a ball or the extent of an area in which a ball is to be dropped. Equipment includes a golf cart, whether or not motorized. If such a cart is shared by two or more players, the cart and everything in it are deemed to be the equipment of the player whose ball is involved except that, when the cart is being moved by one of the players sharing it, the cart and everything in it are deemed to be that player's equipment. Note: A ball played at the hole being played is equipment when it has been lifted and not put back into play.

Equipment touches, moves, stops, deflects ball
- *Three-Ball Match Play*

- *Artificial Devices and Unusual Equipment*

Error

- *Wrong information*

Estimated original position of ball

- *Procedure When Play Resumed*

Etiquette

- *Care of the Course*
- *Committee*

- *Consideration for Other Players*
- *Pace of Play*
- *Penalties for Breach of Etiquette*
- *Priority on the Course*
- *Safety*
- *The Spirit of the Game*

Examine the ball

- *Ball Unfit for Play*

Exceed 14 clubs

- *Maximum of 14 Clubs*

Exceptions

- *Committee*

Excess Clubs

- *Maximum of 14 Clubs*

Exchange balls

- *Wrong Ball*

Exclude the operation of any Rule

- *Agreement to Waive Rules*

Executive Committee

- *Amateurism*
- *Procedure for Enforcement of the Rules*

Exerting Influence on Ball (Rule 1–2)

- <u>Player or caddie MUST NOT</u>: A player or caddie must not take any action to influence the position or the movement of a ball except in accordance with the Rules.

- <u>Penalty for Breach of Rule</u>: *Match play*, loss of hole; *Stroke play*, two strokes.

- <u>Serious breach</u>: In the case of a serious breach of this Rule, the Committee may impose a penalty of DISQUALIFICATION.

- *By Opponent, Caddie or Equipment in Match Play*
- *Game*
- *Movable Obstruction*
- *Three-Ball Match Play*

Exhibition

- *Expenses*
- *Prizes*
- *Use of Golf Skill or Reputation*

Expenses

<u>MAY NOT</u> receive reimbursement

- Except as provided in the Rules, an amateur golfer must not accept expenses, in money or otherwise, from any source to play in a golf competition or exhibition.

MAY receive reimbursement

An amateur golfer may receive reasonable expenses, not exceeding the actual expenses incurred, to play in a golf competition or exhibition as follows:

- Family Support: An amateur golfer may receive expenses from a member of his family or a legal guardian.

- Junior Golfers: A junior golfer may receive expenses when competing in a competition limited exclusively to junior golfers.

- Individual Events: An amateur golfer may receive expenses when competing in individual events, provided he complies with the following provisions:

  (i) Where the competition is to take place in the United States, the expenses must be approved by and paid through the player's state or regional golf association.

  (ii) Where the competition is to take place in another country, the expenses must be approved by both the USGA and the national union or association in the country in which the competition is to be staged. The expenses must be paid through the player's state or regional golf association, or, subject to the approval of the USGA, by the body controlling golf in the territory he is visiting.

The USGA may limit the receipt of expenses to a specific number of competitive days in any one calendar year, and an amateur golfer must not exceed any such limit. In such a case, the expenses are deemed to include reasonable travel time and practice days in connection with the competitive days.

Exception: An amateur golfer must not receive expenses, directly or indirectly, from a professional agent or any other similar source as may be determined by the USGA.

<u>No promotion</u>: An amateur golfer of golf skill or reputation must not promote or advertise the source of any expenses received (see Rule *Use of Golf Skill or Reputation*).

- <u>Team Events</u>: An amateur golfer, may receive expenses when he is representing the following in a team competition, practice session or training camp:

  his country,
  his state or regional golf association,
  his golf club,
  his business or industry, or
  a similar body (includes a recognized educational institution or military service)

  Unless otherwise stated, the expenses must be paid by the body that the amateur golfer is representing or the body controlling golf in the country he is visiting.

- <u>Invitation Unrelated to Golf Skill</u>: An amateur golfer who is invited for reasons unrelated to golf skill (e.g., a celebrity, a business associate or customer) to take part in a golf event may receive expenses.

- <u>Exhibitions</u>: An amateur golfer who is participating in an exhibition in aid of a recognized charity may receive expenses, provided that the exhibition is not run in connection with another golfing event in which the player is competing.

- <u>Sponsored Handicap Competitions</u>: An amateur golfer may receive expenses when competing in a sponsored handicap competition, provided the competition has been approved as follows:

  (i) Where the competition is to take place in the United States, the annual approval of the USGA must first be obtained in advance by the sponsor; and

  (ii) Where the competition is to take place in more than one country or involves golfers from another country, the approval of the USGA and the national union of the other country must first be obtained in advance by the sponsor. The application for this approval should be sent to the national union in the country where the competition commences when it does not commence in the United States.

- *Amateur Status*
- *Prizes*
- *Use of Golf Skill or Reputation*

Extended period

- *Committee*

Extension of line of play

- *Improving lie, swing, or line of play*

External attachments

- *Clubs*

Extra Club(s)

- *Clubs*

F

Face

- *Club Face*
- *Clubhead*
- *Foreign Material*

Failure to:

Complete the play of a hole
- *Four-Ball Stroke Play*

Hole Out (*Stroke Play*) **(Rule 3–2)**
- If a competitor fails to hole out at any hole and does not correct his mistake before he makes a stroke on the next teeing ground or, in the case of the last hole of the round, before he leaves the putting green, he is DISQUALIFIED.

Include a penalty
- *Disputes and Decisions*
- *Information as to Strokes Taken*

Inform his opponent
- *Information as to Strokes Taken*

Fair strike at the ball

- *Striking the ball*

Fairway

- *Embedded Ball*

Falling

- *Ball Falling Off Tee*
- *Ball in Hazard*

Falls to pieces (ball)

- *Unfit for Play*

Family Support

- *Expenses*

Farthest from the hole

- *Order of Play*

Feathers

- *Loose Impediments*

Feet firmly planted

- *Stance*

Fellow-Competitor

- *Competitor*

Fence

- <u>Out-of-Bounds</u>: Out–of–bounds marked by INSIDE point of fence.

Fewer than 14 clubs

- *Maximum of 14 Clubs*

Fewest strokes

- *Winner* (stroke play)

Final decision

- *Committee Decision*
- *Disputes and Decisions*
- *Procedure for Enforcement of the Rules*

Financial gain or incentive

- *Gambling*
- *Use of Golf Skill or Reputation*

Find ball

- *Searching for Ball*

Finger test

- *Club Face*

Fins (club)

- *Clubhead*

First provisional ball

- *Provisional Ball*

First to play

- *Order of Play*

Flagstick (Rule 17)

- Definition: The *flagstick* is a movable straight indicator, with or without bunting or other material attached, centered in the hole to show its position. It must be circular in cross–section. Padding or shock absorbent material that might unduly influence the movement of the ball is prohibited.

- *Ball Resting Against Flagstick*
- *Ball Striking Flagstick or Attendant*
- *Flagstick Attended, Removed or Held Up*
- *Line of Play*
- *Unauthorized Attendance*

Flagstick Attended, Removed or Held Up (Rule 17–1)

- OK before making a stroke: Before making a stroke from anywhere on the course, the player may have the flagstick attended, removed or held up to indicate the position of the hole.

- NOT during/after stroke: If the flagstick is not attended, removed or held up before the player makes a stroke, it must not be attended, removed or held up during the stroke or while the player's ball is in motion if doing so might influence the movement of the ball.

- <u>Standing near flagstick is attending</u>: If the flagstick is in the hole and anyone stands near it while a stroke is being made, he is deemed to be attending the flagstick.

- <u>Player may object to attending flagstick</u>: If, prior to the stroke, the flagstick is attended, removed or held up by anyone with the player's knowledge and he makes no objection, the player is deemed to have authorized it.

- <u>Attends flagstick while stroke being made</u>: If anyone attends or holds up the flagstick while a stroke is being made, he is deemed to be attending the flagstick until the ball comes to rest.

- *Advice*
- *Flagstick*

Foot touching the line of putt

- *Standing Astride or on Line of Putt*

For the Hole Only

- *Four-Ball Stroke Play*

Forecaddie

- <u>Definition</u>: A *forecaddie* is one who is employed by the Committee to indicate to players the position of balls during play. He is an outside agency.

Foreign country

- *Expenses*

Foreign Material

Ball (Rule 5–2)

- <u>Not applied to ball</u>: Foreign material must not be applied to a ball for the purpose of changing its playing characteristics.

- <u>Penalty for breach of Rule</u>: DISQUALIFICATION.

- *Ball*
- *Playing Characteristics Changed*

Clubs (Rule 4–2b)

- <u>Not applied to club</u>: Foreign material must not be applied to the club face for the purpose of influencing the movement of the ball.

- <u>Penalty for Breach of Rule</u>: DISQULAIFICATION.

- *Clubs*

Forfeit

- *Amateurism*
- *Procedure for Enforcement of the Rules* (Amateurism)

Form and Make of Clubs (Rule 4–1)

- <u>Conform to Specifications</u>: The player's clubs must conform with this Rule and the provisions, specifications and interpretations set forth in Appendix II. A club that conforms with the Rules when new is deemed to conform after wear through normal use.

- <u>Altered club must conform</u>: Any part of a club that has been purposely altered is regarded as new and must, in its altered state, conform with the Rules.

- *Clubs*

Forms of gambling

- *Gambling*

Four-Ball

Match Play

- *Best-Ball and Four-Ball Match Play*
- *Match*

Stroke Play (Rule 31)

- <u>General</u>: (Rule 31–1) In four–ball stroke play two competitors play as partners, each playing his own ball. The lower score of the partners is the score for the hole. If one partner fails to complete the play of a hole, there is no penalty. The Rules of Golf, so far as they are not at variance with the following specific Rules, apply to four–ball stroke play.

- <u>Representation of Side</u>: (Rule 31–2) A side may be represented by either partner for all or any part of a stipulated round; both partners need not be present. An absent competitor may join his partner between holes, but not during play of a hole.

- <u>Maximum of 14 Clubs</u>: (Rule 31–3) The side is penalized for a breach of Rules *Damaged Clubs* and *Maximum of 14 Clubs* by either partner.

- <u>Scoring</u>: (Rule 31–4) The marker is required to record for each hole only the gross score of whichever partner's score is to count. The gross scores to count must be individually identifiable; otherwise the side is disqualified. Only one of the partners need be responsible for complying with Rule *Stroke Play* (see *Disqualification Penalties—Breach by One Partner* below).

- <u>Order of Play</u>: (Rule 31–5) Balls belonging to the same side may be played in the order the side considers best.

- <u>Wrong Ball</u>: (Rule 31–6) If a competitor makes a stroke at a wrong ball that is not in a hazard, he incurs a penalty of two strokes and must correct his mistake by playing the correct ball or by proceeding under the Rules. His partner incurs no penalty even if the wrong ball belongs to him. If the wrong ball belongs to another competitor, its owner must place a ball on the spot from which the wrong ball was first played.

- <u>Disqualification Penalties</u>: (Rule 31–7)

   Breach by One Partner

   A side is disqualified from the competition for a breach of any of the following by either partner:

   Agreement to Waive Rules
   Artificial Devices and Unusual Equipment
   Caddie (more than one; failure to correct breach)
   Clubs
   Handicap (playing off higher handicap; failure to record handicap)
   Practice Before or Between Rounds
   Refusal to Comply with a Rule
   Signing and Returning Scorecard
   The Ball
   Undue Delay; Slow Play (repeated offense)
   Wrong Score for Hole—when the recorded score of the partner whose score is to count is lower than actually taken. If the recorded score of the partner whose score is to count is higher than actually taken, it must stand as returned.

   Breach by Both Partners

   A side is disqualified:

   (i) for a breach by both of Rule *Time of Starting and Groups* or Rule *Discontinuance of Play*, or

(ii) if, at the same hole, each partner is in breach of a Rule the penalty for which is disqualification from the competition or for a hole.

For the Hole Only

In all other cases where a breach of a Rule would result in disqualification, the competitor is disqualified only for the hole at which the breach occurred.

- <u>Effect of Other Penalties</u>: (Rule 31–8) If a competitor's breach of a Rule assists his partner's play, the partner incurs the applicable penalty in addition to any penalty incurred by the competitor. In all other cases where a competitor incurs a penalty for breach of a Rule, the penalty does not apply to his partner.

- *Committee*

Foursomes

- *Committee*
- *Match*
- *Threesomes and Foursomes*

Fourteen Clubs

- *Clubs*
- *Maximum of 14 Clubs*

Frost and dew

- <u>Not casual water</u>: Frost and dew are NOT casual water.

- *Improving Lie, Area of Intended Stance or Swing, or Line of Play*

Fruit

- *Loose Impediments*

Furrows (club)

- *Clubhead*

G

Gain (financial)

- *Use of Golf Skill or Reputation*

Gained a significant advantage

- *Playing from Wrong Place*

Gambling (USGA Policy on Gambling)

General

- Amateurism: An *amateur golfer* is one who plays the game as a non–remunerative and non–profit–making sport. Financial incentive in amateur golf, which can be the result of some forms of gambling or wagering, could give rise to abuse of the Rules both in play and in manipulation of handicaps that would be detrimental to the integrity of the game.

- Cash prizes in competitions: There is a distinction between playing for prize money (Rule *Prizes*), gambling or wagering that is contrary to the purpose and spirit of the Rules (Rule *Other Conduct Incompatible with Amateurism*), and forms of gambling or wagering that do not, of themselves, breach the Rules. An amateur golfer or a Committee in charge of a competition where amateur golfers are competing should consult with the USGA if in any doubt as to the application of the Rules. In the absence of such guidance, it is recommended that no cash prizes be awarded so as to ensure that the Rules are upheld.

Acceptable Forms of Gambling

- <u>Incidental to the game</u>: There is no objection to informal gambling or wagering among individual golfers or teams of golfers when it is incidental to the game. It is not practicable to define informal gambling or wagering precisely, but features that would be consistent with such gambling or wagering include:

  - the players in general know each other;
  - participation in the gambling or wagering is optional and is limited to the players;
  - the sole source of all money won by the players is advanced by the players; and
  - the amount of money involved is not generally considered to be excessive.

Therefore, informal gambling or wagering is acceptable provided the primary purpose is the playing of the game for enjoyment, not for financial gain.

Unacceptable Forms of Gambling

- <u>Compulsory</u>: Other forms of gambling or wagering where there is a requirement for players to participate (e.g. compulsory sweepstakes) or that have the potential to involve considerable sums of money (e.g. calcuttas and auction sweepstakes—where players or teams are sold by auction) are not approved. Otherwise, it is difficult to define unacceptable forms of gambling or wagering precisely, but features that would be consistent with such gambling or wagering include:

  - participation in the gambling or wagering is open to non-players; and
  - the amount of money involved is generally considered to be excessive.

- <u>Endanger amateur status</u>: An amateur golfer's participation in gambling or wagering that is not approved may be considered contrary to the purpose and spirit of the Rules (Rule *Other Conduct Incompatible with Amateurism*) and may endanger his Amateur Status.

- <u>Waive right to prize money</u>: Furthermore, organized events designed or promoted to create cash prizes are not permitted. Golfers participating in such events without first irrevocably waiving their right to prize money are deemed to be playing for prize money, in breach of Rule *Prizes*.

- <u>Betting on professional competitions</u>: The Rules of *Amateur Status* do not apply to betting or gambling by amateur golfers on the results of a competition limited to or specifically organized for professional golfers.

- *Other Conduct Incompatible with Amateurism*

Game (Rule 1)

- *Agreement to Waive Rules*
- *Exerting Influence on Ball*
- *Points Not Covered by Rules*

Gauge or measure distance or conditions

- *Artificial Devices and Unusual Equipment*

Gauze

- *Artificial Devices and Unusual Equipment*

General Penalty

- <u>Stroke Play</u>: The penalty for a breach of a Rule in stroke play is two strokes except when otherwise provided. (**Rule 3–5**)

- <u>Match Play</u>: The penalty for a breach of a Rule in match play is loss of hole except when otherwise provided. (**Rule 2–6**)

Give advice

- *Advice*

Give strokes (handicap)

- *Committee*

Gloves

- *Artificial Devices and Unusual Equipment*

Golf ball

- *Ball*
- *The Ball*

Golf country club

- *Use of Golf Skill or Reputation*

Golf competitions

- *Amateurism*

Golf equipment

- *Use of Golf Skill or Reputation*

Golf Skill or Reputation

- <u>Definition</u>: Generally, an amateur golfer is only considered to have golf skill if he has had competitive success at the local level or competes at the national level. Golf reputation can only be gained through golf skill and does not include prominence for service to the game of golf as an administrator. It is a matter for the USGA to decide whether a particular amateur golfer has golf skill or reputation.

Golfers Organization

- *Professionalism*

Grants

- *Use of Golf Skill or Reputation*

Grass

- *Bending grass, limbs, objects*

Green

- *Abnormal Ground Conditions* (diagram "puddle on green")
- *Wrong Putting Green*

Grip

- <u>Definition</u>: The grip consists of material added to the shaft to enable the player to obtain a firm hold. The grip must be straight and plain in form, must extend to the end of the shaft and must not be molded for any part of the hands. If no material is added, that portion of the shaft designed to be held by the player must be considered the grip.

- Circular: For clubs other than putters the grip must be circular in cross–section, except that a continuous, straight, slightly raised rib may be incorporated along the full length of the grip, and a slightly indented spiral is permitted on a wrapped grip or a replica of one.

- Maximum cross-section: The grip may be tapered but must not have any bulge or waist. Its cross–sectional dimensions measured in any direction must not exceed 1.75 inches (44.45 mm).

- Axis: For clubs other than putters the axis of the grip must coincide with the axis of the shaft.

- Putter: A putter grip may have a non–circular cross–section, provided the cross–section has no concavity, is symmetrical and remains generally similar throughout the length of the grip. A putter may have two grips provided each is circular in cross–section, the axis of each coincides with the axis of the shaft, and they are separated by at least 1.5 inches (38.1 mm).

- *Artificial Devices and Unusual Equipment*
- *Clubs*
- *Damaged Clubs* (grip becomes loose)
- *Design*

Gripping the club

- *Artificial Devices and Unusual Equipment*

Grooves

- *Club Face*

Gross score

- *Four-Ball Stroke Play*

Ground Conditions

- *Abnormal Ground Conditions*

Ground Under Repair

(relief diagram under *Abnormal Ground Conditions*)

- <u>Definition</u>: *Ground under repair* is any part of the course so marked by order of the Committee or so declared by its authorized representative. It includes material piled for removal and a hole made by a green keeper, even if not so marked.

- <u>Boundaries</u>: All ground and any grass, bush, tree or other growing thing within the ground under repair is part of the ground under repair. The margin of ground under repair extends vertically downward, but not upward. Stakes and lines defining ground under repair [usually blue] are in such ground. Such stakes are obstructions. A ball is in ground under repair when it lies in or any part of it touches the ground under repair.

- <u>Material abandoned but not intended to be removed</u>: Grass cuttings and other material left on the course that have been abandoned and are not intended to be removed are not ground under repair unless so marked.

- <u>Local Rule</u>: The Committee may make a Local Rule prohibiting play from ground under repair or an environmentally–sensitive area defined as ground under repair.

- *Abnormal Ground Conditions* (see diagram)
- *Committee*

Ground your club

- After taking a stance, you have *addressed the ball*.

- DO NOT ground your club in a trap.

- *Ball in Hazard*
- *Improving Lie, Area of Intended Stance or Swing, or Line of Play* (grounded only lightly)

Groups

- *Committee*
- *Time of Starting and Groups*

Guidelines for pace of play

- *Undue Delay; Slow Play*

Guilty of a serious breach of etiquette

- *Committee*

H

Halved Hole (Rule 2–2)

- A hole is halved if each side holes out in the same number of strokes.

- When a player has holed out and his opponent has been left with a stroke for the half, if the player subsequently incurs a penalty, the hole is halved.

- *Committee* (halved match)
- *Match Play*

Hand

- *Ball in Hazard*

Handicap (Rule 6–2)

- <u>Match Play</u>—Before starting a match in a handicap competition, the players should determine from one another their respective handicaps. If a player begins a match having declared a handicap higher than that to which he is entitled and this affects the number of strokes given or received, he is disqualified; otherwise, the player must play off the declared handicap.

- <u>Stroke Play</u>—In any round of a handicap competition, the competitor must ensure that his handicap is recorded on his Scorecard before it is returned to the Committee. If no handicap is recorded on his Scorecard before it is returned, or if the recorded handicap is higher than that to which he is entitled and this affects the number of strokes received, he is disqualified from the handicap competition; otherwise, the score stands.

- <u>Player's responsibility</u>: It is the player's responsibility to know the holes at which handicap strokes are to be given or received.

- *Best-Ball and Four-Ball Match Play*
- *Bogey and Par Competitions*
- *Committee* (handicap holes; stroke table)
- *Disputes and Decisions*
- *Expenses* (amateur)
- *Four-Ball Stroke Play*
- *Gambling*
- *Stroke Play*
- *Stableford Competitions*
- *The Player*
- *Winner* (stroke play)

Handkerchief

- *Artificial Devices and Unusual Equipment*

Handle loose impediment

- *Ball in Hazard*

Hazards

- <u>Definition</u>: A *hazard* is any bunker or water hazard. The boundary extends upward and downward

- *Ball in Hazard*
- *Ball Played Within Water Hazard*
- *Loose Impediments*
- *Relief for Ball in Water Hazard*

Head

- *Clubhead*
- *Clubs*

Heel

- *Clubhead*
- *Clubs*

Held Up (flagstick)

- *Flagstick Attended, Removed or Held Up*

Help

- *Line of Play*

Higher score

- *Scoring and Scorecard*

Highest number of points

- *Stableford Competitions*

Hit provisional ball

- *Provisional Ball*

Hole

- <u>Definition</u>: The *hole* must be 4–1/4 inches (108 mm) in diameter and at least 4 inches (101.6 mm) deep. If a lining is used, it must be sunk at least 1 inch (25.4 mm) below the putting green surface unless the nature of the soil makes it impracticable to do so; its outer diameter must not exceed 4 1/4 inches (108 mm).

- *Ball Overhanging Hole*
- *Committee* (hole cuts)
- *Repair of Hole Plugs*

Holed out

- <u>Definition</u>: A ball is *holed* when it is at rest within the circumference of the hole and all of it is below the level of the lip of the hole.

- *Concession of Next Stroke, Hole or Match*
- *Failure to Hole Out*
- *Halved Hole*

Hole-In-One Prizes

- *Prizes* (amateur)

Holes (play)

- *Committee* (holes handicapped)
- *Match Play* (holes up)
- *Order of Play—Match Play* (hole has been halved)
- *Stableford Competitions* (hole played in points)

Honor

- <u>Definition</u>: The player who is to play first from the teeing ground is said to have the *honor*.

- *Order of Play* (Match Play)
- *Order of Play* (Stroke Play)
- *Playing out of turn*

I

Ice and Snow

- <u>Casual water OR loose impediments</u>: Ice and snow can be casual water OR loose impediments, whichever the player chooses.

- *Manufactured Ice*

Identifying Ball (Rule 12–2)

- <u>Identification mark on ball</u>: The responsibility for playing the proper ball rests with the player. Each player should put an identification mark on his ball.

- <u>Lift the ball to identify</u>: Except in a hazard, if a player has reason to believe a ball is his, he may lift the ball without penalty to identify it. Before lifting the ball, the player must announce his intention to his opponent in match play or his marker or a fellow–competitor in stroke play and mark the position of the ball. He may then lift the ball and identify it provided that he gives his opponent, marker or fellow–competitor an opportunity to observe the lifting and replacement. The ball must not be cleaned beyond the extent necessary for identification when lifted. If the player fails to comply with all or any part of this procedure, or if he lifts his ball for identification in a hazard, he incurs a penalty of one stroke.

- <u>Replace your own ball</u>: If the lifted ball is the player's ball he must replace it. If he fails to do so, he incurs the general penalty.

- <u>Penalty</u>: *Match Play*, Loss of hole; *Stroke Play*, Two strokes.

- *Ball*
- *Mark the ball*
- *Searching for Ball*

Ignored Rules

- <u>Disqualification</u>: Both players in *Match play*; all players in *Stroke play*.

Illness

- *Discontinuance of Play*
- *Resumption of Play*

Immovable Obstruction (Rule 24–2)

Interference

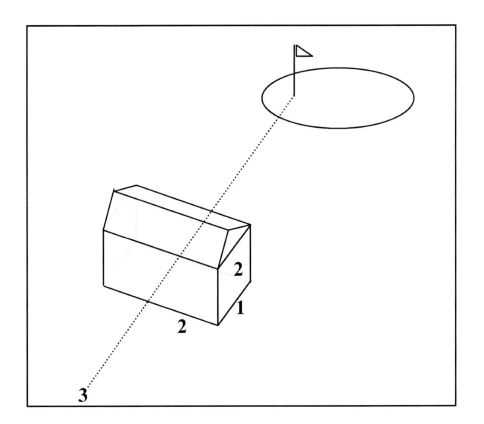

- <u>Definition</u>: Interference by an immovable obstruction occurs when a ball lies in or on the obstruction, or when the obstruction [1—**interferes with the player's stance**] or the [2—**area of his intended swing** (backswing and follow through)].

- <u>Putting green</u>: If the player's ball lies on the putting green, interference also occurs if an immovable obstruction on the putting green intervenes on his line of putt. Otherwise, [3—**intervention on the line of play is not, of itself, interference under this Rule**].

Relief (see diagram at *Cart Path*)

- Except when the ball is in a water hazard or a lateral water hazard, a player may take relief from interference by an immovable obstruction as follows:

  (i) <u>Through the Green</u>: If the ball lies through the green, the player must lift the ball and drop it without penalty within one club-length of and not nearer the hole than the nearest point of relief. The nearest point of relief must not be in a hazard or on a putting green. When the ball is dropped within one club-length of the nearest point of relief, the ball must first strike a part of the course at a spot that avoids interference by the immovable obstruction and is not in a hazard and not on a putting green. (cart path)

  (ii) <u>In a Bunker</u>: If the ball is in a bunker, the player must lift the ball and drop it either:

    (a) <u>Without penalty</u>, in accordance with Clause (i) above, except that the nearest point of relief must be in the bunker and the ball must be dropped in the bunker; or

    (b) <u>Under penalty</u> of one stroke, outside the bunker keeping the point where the ball lay directly between the hole and the spot on which the ball is dropped, with no limit to how far behind the bunker the ball may be dropped.

  (iii) <u>On the Putting Green</u>: If the ball lies on the putting green, the player must lift the ball and place it without penalty at the nearest point of relief that is not in a hazard. The nearest point of relief may be off the putting green.

(iv) <u>On the Teeing Ground</u>: If the ball lies on the teeing ground, the player must lift the ball and drop it without penalty in accordance with Clause (i) above.

- <u>Clean ball</u>: The ball may be cleaned when lifted under this Rule.

- <u>Ball rolls</u>: If the ball rolls to a position where there is interference by the condition from which relief was taken, see Rule *Dropping and Re-Dropping* (When to Re–Drop).

- <u>Exception</u>: A player may not take relief under this Rule if (a) it is clearly unreasonable for him to make a stroke because of interference by anything other than an immovable obstruction or (b) interference by an immovable obstruction would occur only through use of an unnecessarily abnormal stance, swing or direction of play.

- <u>Water hazard</u>: If a ball is in a water hazard (including a lateral water hazard), the player may not take relief from interference by an immovable obstruction. The player must play the ball as it lies or proceed under Rule *Relief for Ball in Water Hazard*.

- <u>Ball not recoverable</u>: If a ball to be dropped or placed under this Rule is not immediately recoverable, another ball may be substituted.

- <u>Local rule</u>: The Committee may make a Local Rule stating that the player must determine the nearest point of relief without crossing over, through or under the obstruction.

- *Ball Lost in Obstruction*
- *Cart path* (diagram)
- *Improving Lie, Area of Intended Stance or Swing, or Line of Play*
- *Obstructions*

Impact area

- *Club Face*

Impact of a ball

- *Repair of Hole Plugs*

Impediments

- *Ball in Hazard*
- *Loose Impediments*

Improving Lie, Area of Intended Stance or Swing, or Line of Play (Rule 13–2)

- <u>A player must not improve or allow to be improved</u>:

  (a) the position or lie of his ball;

  (b) the area of his intended stance or swing;

  (c) his line of play or a reasonable extension of that line beyond the hole; or

  (d) the area in which he is to drop or place a ball......<u>by any of the following actions</u>:

  (i) moving, bending or breaking anything growing or fixed (including immovable obstructions and objects defining out of bounds);

  (ii) creating or eliminating irregularities of surface;

(iii) removing or pressing down sand, loose soil, replaced divots or other cut turf placed in position; or

(iv) removing dew, frost or water.

- <u>Incurs no penalty</u>: However, the player incurs no penalty if the action occurs:

  (a) in fairly taking his stance;

  (b) in making a stroke or the backward movement of his club for a stroke and the stroke is made;

  (c) on the teeing ground in creating or eliminating irregularities of surface; or

  (d) on the putting green in removing sand and loose soil or in repairing damage.

- <u>Club grounded slightly</u>: The club may be grounded only lightly and must not be pressed on the ground.

- *Ball Played as it Lies*
- *Indicating Line of Play*
- *Stance*

In a Bunker

- *Ball Lost in Obstruction*

In a Water Hazard

- *Ball Lost in Obstruction*

In Bounds

- If your ball is in–bounds, you can stand out–of–bounds to play it.

In Play

- *When Ball Dropped or Placed is in Play*

Incidental to the game

- *Gambling*

Incorrect information

- *Information as to Strokes Taken*

Incorrect order

- *Threesomes and Foursomes*

Incorrectly Substituted, Dropped or Placed (ball)

- *Lifting Ball Incorrectly Substituted, Dropped or Placed*
- *When Ball Dropped or Placed is in Play*

Incurred a penalty

- *Information as to Strokes Taken*

Indicating Line of Play (Rule 8–2)

- <u>Other Than on Putting Green</u>: Except on the putting green, a player may have the line of play indicated to him by anyone, but no one may be positioned by the player on or close to the line or an extension of the line beyond the hole while the stroke is being made. Any mark placed by the player or with his knowledge to indicate the line must be removed before the stroke is made.

Exception: Flagstick attended or held up (see *Flagstick Attended, Removed or Held Up* to indicate the position of the hole).

- On the Putting Green: When the player's ball is on the putting green, the player, his partner or either of their caddies may, before but not during the stroke, point out a line for putting, but in so doing the putting green must not be touched. A mark must not be placed anywhere to indicate a line for putting (see *Touching Line of Putt*).

- Penalty for Breach of Rule: *Match Play*, Loss of hole; *Stroke Play*, Two strokes.

- Teams: The Committee may, in the conditions of a team competition, permit each team to appoint one person who may give advice (including pointing out a line for putting) to members of that team. The Committee may establish conditions relating to the appointment and permitted conduct of that person, who must be identified to the Committee before giving advice.

- *Advice*

Inducement to play for that club or course

- *Use of Golf Skill or Reputation*

Ineligible

- *Amateurism*

Influence the position or the movement of a ball

- *Exerting Influence on Ball*
- *Flagstick Attended, Removed or Held Up*
- *Foreign Material*

Inform

Marker
- *Information as to Strokes Taken*

Opponent
- *Penalties*
- *Provisional Ball*

Informal gambling

- *Gambling*

Information as to Strokes Taken (Rule 9)

- <u>General</u>: The number of strokes a player has taken includes any penalty strokes incurred. (Rule 9–1)

- <u>Match Play</u>: (Rule 9–2) An opponent is entitled to ascertain from the player, during the play of a hole, the number of strokes he has taken and, after play of a hole, the number of strokes taken on the hole just completed. <u>Wrong Information</u>: A player must not give wrong information to his opponent. If a player gives wrong information, he loses the hole. A player is deemed to have given wrong information if he:

  (i) fails to inform his opponent as soon as practicable that he has incurred a penalty, unless (a) he was obviously proceeding under a Rule involving a penalty and this was observed by his opponent, or (b) he corrects the mistake before his opponent makes his next stroke; or

  (ii) gives incorrect information during play of a hole regarding the number of strokes taken and does not correct the mistake before his opponent makes his next stroke; or

(iii) gives incorrect information regarding the number of strokes taken to complete a hole and this affects the opponent's understanding of the result of the hole, unless he corrects the mistake before any player makes a stroke from the next teeing ground or, in the case of the last hole of the match, before all players leave the putting green. A player has given wrong information even if it is due to the failure to include a penalty that he did not know he had incurred. It is the player's responsibility to know the Rules.

- <u>Stroke Play</u>: (Rule 9–3) A competitor who has incurred a penalty should inform his marker as soon as practicable.

Infringing the Rules

- *Reinstatement of Amateur Status*

Initial Velocity

- *The Ball*

Insects

- *By Outside Agency*
- *Loose Impediments*

Inside the teeing ground

- *Playing outside the teeing ground*

Instruction

- <u>Definition</u>: *Instruction* covers the physical aspects of playing golf, i.e., the actual mechanics of swinging a golf club and hitting a golf ball. Instruction does not cover the psychological aspects of the game or the Rules or Etiquette of Golf.

General

- <u>No payment for instruction</u>: Except as provided in the Rules, an amateur golfer must not receive payment or compensation, directly or indirectly, for giving instruction in playing golf.

Where Payment Permitted

- <u>Schools, Colleges, Camps</u>: An amateur golfer who is (i) an employee of an educational institution or system or (ii) a counselor at a camp or other similar organized program may receive payment or compensation for golf Instruction to students in the institution, system or camp, provided that the total time devoted to golf Instruction comprises less than 50 percent of the time spent in the performance of all duties as such an employee or counselor.

- <u>Approved Programs</u>: An amateur golfer may receive expenses, payment or compensation for giving golf Instruction as part of a program that has been approved in advance by the USGA.

Instruction in Writing

- <u>Written golf instruction OK</u>: An amateur golfer may receive payment or compensation for golf instruction in writing, provided his ability or reputation as a golfer was not a major factor in his employment or in the commission or sale of his work.

- *Amateur Status*

Interference

- *Abnormal Ground Conditions*
- *Ball Interfering with Play*
- *Committee* (interferes with the proper playing of the game)
- *Immovable Obstruction*

- *Lifting and Marking* (ball–marker interferes with play)
- *Tee-Markers* (interference with stance)
- *Wrong Putting Green*

Interpretations of the Rules

- *Artificial Devices and Unusual Equipment*

Intervenes on line of putt (obstruction)

- *Immovable Obstruction*

Investigation

- *Procedure for Enforcement of the Rules*

Invitation Unrelated to Golf Skill

- *Expenses*

Irons

- *Clubhead*
- *Clubs*

Irregularities of surface

- *Improving Lie, Area of Intended Stance or Swing, or Line of Play*

J

Join a match

- *Best-Ball and Four-Ball Match Play*

Join partner between holes

- *Four-Ball Stroke Play*

Junior Golfer

- <u>Definition</u>: A *junior golfer* is an amateur golfer who has not yet reached:

   (i) the September 1 following graduation from secondary school; or

   (ii) his 19th birthday, whichever shall come first.

- *Expenses*

K

Keeping Score

- *Marker*

Knew before the competition closed

- *Disputes and Decisions*

Knobs (club)

- *Clubhead*

Knock the ball off the tee

- *Ball falling off the tee*

L

Last hole

- *Wrong Information*

Later claim

- *Doubt as to Procedure; Disputes and Claims*

Lateral Water Hazard

- <u>Definition</u>: A *lateral water hazard* is a water hazard or that part of a water hazard so situated that it is not possible or is deemed by the Committee to be impracticable to drop a ball behind the water hazard in accordance with Rule *Relief for Ball in Water Hazard*. That part of a water hazard to be played as a lateral water hazard should be distinctively marked. A ball is in a lateral water hazard when it lies in or any part of it touches the lateral water hazard.

- <u>Red stakes or lines</u>: Stakes or lines used to define a lateral water hazard must be red. When both stakes and lines are used to define lateral water hazards, the stakes identify the hazard and the lines define the hazard margin.

- <u>Committee may make Local Rules</u>: The Committee may make a Local Rule prohibiting play from an environmentally–sensitive area defined as a lateral water hazard. The Committee may define a lateral water hazard as a water hazard.

- *Ball Lost in Obstruction*
- *Ball Played Within Water Hazard*
- *Relief for Ball in Water Hazard*

Leaves

- *Loose Impediments*

Leaving the course

- *Discontinuance of Play; Resumption of Play*

Legal guardian

- *Expenses*

Lending Name or Likeness

- *Use of Golf Skill or Reputation*

Length of...

- *Club Face* (grooves)
- *Clubs*

Lie Altered

- *Ball Moved in Measuring* (Ball at Rest Moved)

Lie angle

- *Clubhead*

Lie of Ball

- *Ball in Hazard*

- *Improving Lie, Area of Intended Stance or Swing, or Line of Play*
- *Placing and Replacing*
- *Wrong Ball* (lie of ball to be placed or replaced altered)

Lie of club

- *Damaged Clubs*

Lifting and Cleaning Ball (Rule 16–1b)

- <u>Ball on the putting green may be lifted</u>: A ball on the putting green may be lifted and, if desired, cleaned. The position of the ball must be marked before it is lifted and the ball must be replaced.

- *Ball Unplayable*
- *Embedded Ball*
- *Cleaning Ball*
- *Lifting and Marking*
- *Lifting the Ball*
- *Putting Green*
- *Relief for Ball in Water Hazard*

Lifting and Marking (Rule 20–1)

- <u>Ball may be lifted by another person authorized by player</u>: A ball to be lifted under the Rules may be lifted by the player, his partner or another person authorized by the player. In any such case, the player is responsible for any breach of the Rules.

- <u>Ball marked before lifted</u>: The position of the ball must be marked before it is lifted under a Rule that requires it to be replaced. If it is not marked, the player incurs a penalty of one stroke and the ball must be replaced. If it is not replaced, the player incurs the general penalty for breach of this Rule, but there is no additional penalty under this Rule

- <u>Mark behind ball</u>: The position of a ball to be lifted should be marked by placing a ball–marker, a small coin or other similar object immediately behind the ball.

- <u>Move mark interfering with play</u>: If the ball–marker interferes with the play, stance or stroke of another player, it should be placed one or more clubhead–lengths to one side.

- <u>Ball or ball-marker accidentally moved</u>: If a ball or ball–marker is accidentally moved in the process of lifting the ball under a Rule or marking its position, the ball or ball–marker must be replaced. There is no penalty provided the movement of the ball or ball–marker is directly attributable to the specific act of marking the position of or lifting the ball. Otherwise, the player incurs a penalty of one stroke under this Rule or Rule *By Player, Partner, Caddie or Equipment.*

- <u>No additional penalty</u>: If a player incurs a penalty for failing to act in accordance with Rule *Ball Unfit for Play* or *Identifying Ball*, there is no additional penalty under this Rule.

- *Lifting and Cleaning Ball*
- *Lifting the Ball, Dropping and Placing*

Lifting Ball Incorrectly Substituted, Dropped or Placed (Rule 20–6)

- <u>Proceed correctly without penalty</u>: A ball incorrectly substituted, dropped or placed in a wrong place or otherwise not in accordance with the Rules but not played may be lifted, without penalty, and the player must then proceed correctly.

- *Lifting the Ball, Dropping, Placing*
- *Playing from Wrong Place*

Lifting Ball When Play Discontinued (Rule 6–8c)

- Suspended play: When a player discontinues play of a hole, he may lift his ball without penalty only if the Committee has suspended play or there is a good reason to lift it.

- Mark before lifting: Before lifting the ball the player must mark its position. If the player discontinues play and lifts his ball without specific permission from the Committee, he must, when reporting to the Committee, report the lifting of the ball.

- Penalty for Breach of Rule: If the player lifts the ball without a good reason to do so, fails to mark the position of the ball before lifting it or fails to report the lifting of the ball, he incurs a penalty of one stroke.

- *Discontinuance of Play*
- *The Player*

Lifting, Dropping and Placing; Playing from Wrong Place (Rule 20)

- *Ball Assisting Play*
- *Ball Interfering with Play*
- *Ball Unfit for Play*
- *By Player, Partner, Caddie or Equipment (Ball at Rest Moved)*
- *Dropping and Re-Dropping*
- *Identifying Ball*
- *Lifting and Cleaning Ball*
- *Lifting and Marking*
- *Lifting Ball Incorrectly Substituted, Dropped or Placed*
- *Making Next Stroke from Where Previous Stroke Made*
- *Movable Obstruction*
- *Placing and Replacing*
- *Playing from Wrong Place*
- *Touching Line of Putt*
- *When Ball Dropped or Placed is in Play*
- *Wrong Putting Green*

Lightning

- *Discontinuance of Play*
- *Resumption of Play*

Likeness

- *Use of Golf Skill or Reputation*

Limbs

- *Bending grass, limbs, objects*

Limit a referee's duties

- *Committee*

Limit for a single award

- *Prizes*

Limit of time

- *Committee*
- *Disputes and Decisions* (time for decisions)

Limit the receipt of expenses

- *Expenses*

Limited to only one caddie

- *Caddie*

Line of Play

- Definition: The *line of play* is the direction that the player wishes his ball to take after a stroke, plus a reasonable distance on either side of the intended direction. The line of play extends vertically upward from the ground, but does not extend beyond the hole.

- *Advice*
- *Assistance* (Striking the Ball)
- *Improving Lie, Area of Intended Stance or Swing, or Line of Play*
- *Indicating Line of Play*

Line of Putt

- Definition: The *line of putt* is the line that the player wishes his ball to take after a stroke on the putting green. Except with respect to Rule *Standing Astride or on Line of Putt*, the line of putt includes a reasonable distance on either side of the intended line. The line of putt does not extend beyond the hole.

- DON'T stand on the line of putt behind the ball.

- DON'T stand on the line of putt behind the hole.

- *Abnormal Ground Conditions*
- *Assistance* (Striking the Ball)
- *Standing Astride or on Line of Putt*
- *Touching Line of Putt*

Lines

- Out–of–bounds marked by INSIDE point of line.

Loose clubhead or grip

- *Damaged Clubs*

Loose Impediments (Rule 23)

- <u>Definition</u>: *Loose impediments* are natural objects including:
  - stones, leaves, twigs, branches and the like,
  - dung, and
  - worms and insects and casts or heaps made by them, provided they are not:
  - fixed or growing,
  - solidly embedded, or
  - adhering to the ball.

- <u>Sand and loose soil</u> are loose impediments ONLY on the putting green, but not elsewhere.

- <u>Snow and natural ice</u>, other than frost, are either casual water or loose impediments, at the option of the player.

- <u>Dew and frost</u> are NOT loose impediments.

Relief (Rule 23–1)

- <u>May be removed</u>: Except when both the loose impediment and the ball lie in or touch the same hazard, any loose impediment may be removed without penalty.

- <u>Ball moves</u>: If the ball lies anywhere other than on the putting green and the removal of a loose impediment by the player causes the ball to move, Rule *By Player, Partner, Caddie or Equipment* applies. <u>On the putting green</u>, if the ball or ball–marker moves in the process of the player removing any loose impediment, the ball or ball–marker must be replaced. There is no penalty provided the movement of the ball or ball–marker is directly attributable to the removal of the loose impediment. Otherwise, if the player causes the ball to move, he incurs a penalty of one stroke under Rule *By Player, Partner, Caddie or Equipment*.

- <u>Ball in motion</u>: When a ball is in motion, a loose impediment that might influence the movement of the ball must not be removed.

- <u>Ball in hazard</u>: If the ball lies in a hazard, the player must not touch or move any loose impediment lying in or touching the same hazard (Rule *Ball in Hazard, Prohibited Actions*).

- <u>Penalty</u>: *Match play*, Loss of hole; *Stroke play*, Two strokes.

- *Ball in Hazard*
- *By Player, Partner, Caddie or Equipment* (Ball at Rest Moved)
- *Improving lie, swing, or line of play* (loose soil)
- *Relief*
- *Searching for Ball*
- *Seeing Ball*
- *Touching line of putt*

Loss of hole

- *Match Play*

Lost Ball

- <u>Definition</u>: A ball is deemed *lost* if:

  a. It is not found or identified as his by the player within five minutes after the player's side or his or their caddies have begun to search for it. NOTE: Time spent in playing a wrong ball is not counted in the five-minute period allowed for search; or

  b. The player has made a stroke at a substituted ball; or

  c. The player has made a stroke at a provisional ball from the place where the original ball is likely to be or from a point nearer the hole than that place.

- <u>Etiquette</u>: If a player believes his ball may be lost outside a water hazard or is out of bounds, to save time, he should play a provisional ball. Players searching for a ball should signal the players in the group behind them to play through as soon as it becomes apparent that the ball will not easily be found. They should not search for five minutes before doing so. Having allowed the group behind to play through, they should not continue play until that group has passed and is out of range.

- *Abnormal Ground Conditions*
- *Ball Lost in Obstruction*
- *Ball Lost or Out of Bounds*
- *Ball Played Within Water Hazard*
- *Provisional Ball*
- *Relief for Ball in Water Hazard* (lost inside or outside the hazard)

Lowest Score

- *Match Play* (Lower net score)
- *Order of Play*
- *Scoring and Scorecard*
- *Winner* (stroke play)

Lying in an abnormal ground condition

- *Searching for Ball*

M

Main body (club)

- *Clubhead*

Make of Clubs

- *Clubs*

Making a stroke

- *Artificial Devices and Unusual Equipment*
- *Improving lie, swing, or line of play*
- *Assistance* (Striking the Ball)
- *Provisional Ball*

Making Next Stroke from Where Previous Stroke Made (Rule 20–5)

- When a player elects or is required to make his next stroke from where a previous stroke was made, he must proceed as follows:

  (a) <u>On the Teeing Ground</u>: The ball to be played must be played from within the teeing ground. It may be played from anywhere within the teeing ground and it may be teed.

  (b) <u>Through the Green and in a Hazard</u>: The ball to be played must be dropped.

  (c) <u>On the Putting Green</u>: The ball to be played must be placed.

- Penalty: *Match play*, Loss of hole; *Stroke play*, Two strokes.

- *Ball Lost or Out of Bounds*
- *Ball Unplayable*
- *Lifting the Ball, Dropping, and Placing*
- *Three-Ball Match Play*
- *Threesomes and Foursomes*

Making Stroke While Another Ball in Motion
(Rule 16–1f)

- No stroke while another ball is in motion: The player must not make a stroke while another ball is in motion after a stroke from the putting green, except that, if a player does so, there is no penalty if it was his turn to play.

- Penalty for Breach of Rule: *Match Play*, Loss of hole; *Stroke Play*, Two strokes.

- *Putting Green*

Manipulation of handicaps

- *Gambling*

Manufactured

- *The Ball*

Manufactured ice

- Is ALWAYS an obstruction.

Manufacturer

- *Artificial Devices and Unusual Equipment*

Margins of water hazards

- *Committee*
- *Water Hazard*

Mark

- *Club Face*

Mark the ball

- <u>Identify your ball</u>: Mark your ball to identify it so that you can continue to play the same ball throughout play.

- *Ball*
- *Ball Unfit for Play*
- *Identifying Ball*
- *Lifting and Cleaning Ball*
- *Lifting and Marking*
- *Lifting Ball When Play Discontinued*

Mark the green

- *Putting Line*

Marker

- <u>Definition</u>: A *marker* is one who is appointed by the Committee to record a competitor's score in stroke play. He may be a fellow–competitor. He is not a referee.

- *Placing and Replacing*

Marking line of play

- *Line of Play*

Markings

- *Club Face*

Match

- <u>Single</u>: A match in which one plays against another.

- <u>Threesome</u>: A match in which one plays against two, and each side plays one ball.

- <u>Foursome</u>: A match in which two play against two, and each side plays one ball.

- <u>Three-Ball</u>: A match–play competition in which three play against one another, each playing his own ball. Each player is playing two distinct matches.

- <u>Best-Ball</u>: A match in which one plays against the better ball of two or the best ball of three players.

- <u>Four-Ball</u>: A match in which two play their better ball against the better ball of two other players.

- *Best-Ball and Four-Ball Match Play* (Match Played Concurrently)
- *Committee* (date)
- *Winner*

Match Play (Rule 2)

- <u>Definition</u>: A match consists of one side playing against another over a stipulated round unless otherwise decreed by the Committee.

- <u>By holes</u>: In match play the game is played by holes.

- <u>Winner of hole</u>: Except as otherwise provided in the Rules, a hole is won by the side that holes its ball in the fewer strokes. In a handicap match the lower net score wins the hole (See *Handicap*).

- <u>State of the match</u>: The state of the match is expressed by the terms: so many *holes up* or *all square*, and so many *to play*.

- <u>Dormie</u>: A side is *dormie* when it is as many holes up as there are holes remaining to be played.

- <u>Penalty</u>: *Match play*, loss of hole.

- *Agreement to Waive Rules*
- *Bogey and Par Competitions*
- *By Opponent, Caddie or Equipment in Match Play*
- *Clubs*
- *Committee*
- *Concession of Next Stroke, Hole or Match*
- *Disputes and Decisions*
- *Doubt as to Procedure; Disputes and Claims*
- *General Penalty*
- *Halved Hole*
- *Penalties*
- *Stableford Competitions*
- *Three-Ball Match Play*
- *Winner*
- *Wrong Ball*
- *Wrong Information*

Material

- *Club Face*

Material added to the shaft

- *Grip*

Material on ball

- *Foreign Material*

Maximum cross-section

- *Grip*

Maximum length of club

- *Clubs*

Maximum of 14 Clubs (Rule 4–4)

- <u>Start with 14 or less</u>: The player must start a stipulated round with not more than 14 clubs. He is limited to the clubs thus selected for that round except that, if he started with fewer than 14 clubs, he may add any number provided his total number does not exceed 14. The addition of a club or clubs must not unduly delay play.

- <u>No borrowing except partners</u>: The player must not add or borrow any club selected for play by any other person playing on the course. <u>Partners</u> may share clubs, provided that the total number of clubs carried by the partners so sharing does not exceed 14.

Penalty for Breach of Rule

- <u>Match play</u>: At the conclusion of the hole at which the breach is discovered, the state of the match is adjusted by deducting one hole for each hole at which a breach occurred. Maximum deduction per round: Two holes.

- <u>Stroke play</u>: Two strokes for each hole at which any breach occurred; maximum penalty per round: Four strokes.

- <u>Extra club(s)</u> *out of play*: Any club or clubs carried or used in breach of Rule must be declared *out of play* by the player to his opponent in match play or his marker or a fellow–competitor in stroke play immediately upon discovery that a breach has occurred. The player must not use the club or clubs for the remainder of the stipulated round. Penalty for breach of this rule is DISQUALIFICATION.

- *Best-Ball and Four-Ball Match Play*
- *Bogey and Par Competitions*
- *Clubs*
- *Four-Ball Stroke Play*
- *Stableford Competitions*

Measurement of clubhead dimensions

- *Clubhead*
- *Clubs*

Measuring

- *Artificial Devices and Unusual Equipment* (measuring distance)
- *Ball Moved in Measuring* (Ball at Rest Moved)
- *By Player, Partner, Caddie or Equipment* (Ball at Rest Moved)
- *Touching Line of Putt*

Members of that team

- *Advice*

Membership

- *Professionalism*
- *Use of Golf Skill or Reputation*

Merchandise

- *Prizes*

Metal

- *Club Face*

Military service

- *Expenses*

Milling

- *Club Face*

Minimum length of club

- *Clubs*

Miss the ball

- <u>Count the stroke</u>: If you move the club forward in an attempt to strike the ball, that is a *stroke* and you must score that stroke, UNLESS, you check your stroke before the clubhead reaches the ball.

Misshapen ball

- *Unfit for Play*

Mistake in number of strokes taken

- *Information as to Strokes Taken*

Mistake is not corrected

- *Substituted Ball*

Modified penalty

- *Disputes and Decisions*

Modify rules

- *Committee*

Molded grip

- *Grip*

Money

- *Expenses*
- *Gambling*
- *Prizes*
- *Professionalism*

More than once

- *Striking the Ball More than Once*

More than one caddie

- *Caddie*

Motion (ball)

- *By Another Ball*
- *By Outside Agency*
- *Making Stroke While Another Ball in Motion*

Movable Obstruction (Rule 24–1)

- Examples: Rake, golf cart, wheelbarrow, bench

- Relief: A player may take relief without penalty from a movable obstruction as follows:

  a. Ball does not lie in or on obstruction: If the ball does not lie in or on the obstruction, the obstruction may be removed. If the ball moves, it must be replaced, and there is no penalty provided that the movement of the ball is directly attributable to the removal of the obstruction. Otherwise, Rule *By Player, Partner, Caddie or Equipment* applies.

b. <u>Ball lies in or on obstruction</u>: If the ball lies in or on the obstruction, the ball may be lifted and the obstruction removed. The ball must through the green or in a hazard be dropped, or on the putting green be placed, as near as possible to the spot directly under the place where the ball lay in or on the obstruction, but not nearer the hole.

- <u>Ball may be cleaned</u>: The ball may be cleaned when lifted under this Rule.

- <u>Ball in motion</u>: When a ball is in motion, an obstruction that might influence the movement of the ball, other than an attended flagstick or equipment of the players, must not be removed.

- <u>Ball not recoverable</u>: If a ball to be dropped or placed under this Rule is not immediately recoverable, another ball may be substituted.

- *Ball Lost in Obstruction*
- *By Player, Partner, Caddie or Equipment* (Ball at Rest Moved)
- *Exerting influence on ball*
- *Obstructions*
- *Relief*
- *Touching Line of Putt*

Move a loose impediment

- *Ball in Hazard*

Move flagstick

- *Ball Resting Against Flagstick*

Move or Moved (ball or ball marker)

- <u>Definition</u>: A ball is deemed to have *moved* if it leaves its position and comes to rest in any other place.

- *Ball Moved in Measuring* (Ball at Rest Moved)
- *By Another Ball* (Ball at Rest Moved)
- *By Fellow-Competitor, Caddie or Equipment in Stroke Play* (Moves the player's ball)
- *By Opponent, Caddie or Equipment in Match Play* (ball at rest moved)
- *By Player, Partner, Caddie or Equipment* (Ball at Rest Moved)
- *Lifting and Marking*
- *Repair of Hole Plugs, Ball Marks, and Other Damage*
- *Searching for Ball*

Move the club

- *Improving lie, swing, or line of play*

Moves tee-marker

- *Tee-Markers*

Moving Ball

- *Playing Moving Ball*

Moving in Water (ball)

- *Ball Moving in Water*
- *Relief for Ball in Water Hazard*

Moving objects

- *Improving Lie, Area of Intended Stance or Swing, or Line of Play*

Moving outside agency

- *By Outside Agency*

Mown area

- *Embedded Ball*

Mud on ball

- *Ball Unfit for Play*

Multiple Awards

- *Prizes*

N

Name

- *Use of Golf Skill or Reputation*

Name of competitor

- *Committee*

National Association for Intercollegiate Athletics

- *Use of Golf Skill or Reputation*

National Collegiate Athletic Association

- *Use of Golf Skill or Reputation*

National Junior College Athletic Association

- *Use of Golf Skill or Reputation*

National prominence

- *Reinstatement of Amateur Status*

Natural objects

- <u>Loose impediment</u>: If NOT fixed, then it is a loose impediment.

Nearest Point of Relief

- <u>Definition</u>: The *nearest point of relief* is the reference point for taking relief without penalty from interference by an immovable obstruction (Rule *Immovable Obstruction*), an abnormal ground condition (Rule *Abnormal Ground Conditions*) or a wrong putting green (Rule *Wrong Putting Green*). It is the point on the course nearest to where the ball lies:

  (i) that is not nearer the hole, and

  (ii) where, if the ball were so positioned, no interference by the condition from which relief is sought would exist for the stroke the player would have made from the original position if the condition were not there.

  <u>Use club to simulate stroke</u>: In order to determine the nearest point of relief accurately, the player should use the club with which he would have made his next stroke if the condition were not there to simulate the address position, direction of play and swing for such a stroke.

- *Immovable Obstruction*

Need not be present

- *Best-Ball and Four-Ball Match Play*

Net score

- *Winner* (stroke play)

New ball

- *Unfit for Play*

New Holes

- *Committee*

Next Stroke

- *Making Next Stroke from Where Previous Stroke Made*

No Disturbance or Distraction

Etiquette

- No movement or noise: Players should always show consideration for other players on the course and should not disturb their play by moving, talking or making unnecessary noise.

- No electronic devices: Players should ensure that any electronic device taken onto the course does not distract other players.

- Wait your turn to tee: On the teeing ground, a player should not tee his ball until it is his turn to play.

- Don't stand close: Players should not stand close to or directly behind the ball, or directly behind the hole, when a player is about to play.

No financial gain

- *Use of Golf Skill or Reputation*

No more than one caddie

- *Caddie*

No referee present

- *Disputes and Decisions*

Non-conforming tee

- *Teeing*

Non-metallic Club Face Markings

- *Club Face*

Non-profit-making

- *Gambling*

Non-remunerative

- *Gambling*

Not allowed to improve

- *Improving lie, swing, or line of play*

Not conforming to Rules

- *Disputes and Decisions*

Not immediately recoverable

- *Immovable Obstruction*

Not present

- *Four-Ball Stroke Play*

Not Recoverable (ball)

- *Ball Moved in Measuring* (Ball at Rest Moved)
- *By Outside Agency*

Notification

- *Procedure for Enforcement of the Rules*

Number of Clubs

- Only 14 can be carried in the bag.

- *Maximum 14 Clubs*

Number of Reinstatements

- *Reinstatement of Amateur Status*

Number of strokes

- *Information as to Strokes Taken*
- *Wrong information*

O

Objects

- *Improving lie, swing, or line of play*

Objects defining out of bounds

- *Improving Lie, Area of Intended Stance or Swing, or Line of Play*

Observe the lifting and replacement

- *Identifying Ball*

Observer

- Definition: An *observer* is one who is appointed by the Committee to assist a referee to decide questions of fact and to report to him any breach of a Rule. An observer should not attend the flagstick, stand at or mark the position of the hole, or lift the ball or mark its position.

Obstructions (Rule 24)

- Definition: An obstruction is <u>anything artificial</u>, including the artificial surfaces and sides of roads and paths and manufactured ice, <u>except</u>:

  a. <u>Objects defining out of bounds</u>, such as walls, fences, stakes and railings;

173

b. Any part of an immovable artificial object that is <u>out of bounds</u>; and

c. Any <u>construction</u> declared by the Committee to be an integral part of the course.

- <u>Movable obstruction</u>: An obstruction is a movable obstruction if it may be (a) moved without unreasonable effort, (b) without unduly delaying play and (c) without causing damage. Otherwise it is an immovable obstruction.

- <u>Local Rule</u>: The Committee may make a Local Rule declaring a movable obstruction to be an immovable obstruction.

- *Ball in Hazard*
- *Ball Lost in Obstruction*
- *Ball Lost or Out of Bounds*
- *Committee*
- *Immovable Obstruction*
- *Improving lie, swing, or line of play*
- *Movable Obstruction*
- *Provisional Ball*

Occupation

- *Use of Golf Skill or Reputation*

Offer of membership

- *Use of Golf Skill or Reputation*

Official course record

- *Course Record*

On the Putting Green

- <u>Etiquette</u>: On the putting green, players should not stand on another player's line of putt or when he is making a stroke, cast a shadow over his line of putt. Players should remain on or close to the putting green until all other players in the group have holed out.

- *Ball Lost in Obstruction*

On time

- *Time of Starting and Groups*

One Caddie at Any One Time

- *Bogey and Par Competitions*
- *Caddie*
- *Stableford Competitions*

One's name or likeness as a player of golf skill or reputation

- *Professionalism*

Opinion

- *Disputes and Decisions*
- *Procedure for Enforcement of the Rules*

Opponent

- *Order of Play—Match Play* (Opponent should have played)
- *Penalties*

- *Second ball*
- *Stroke*
- *Three-Ball Match Play* (Opponent touches, moves, stops, deflects ball)
- *Wrong Information*

Oral agreement with a professional agent or sponsor

- *Professionalism*

Order of handicap holes

- *Committee*

Order of play (Rule 10–3)

- <u>Provisional or second ball</u>: If a player plays a provisional ball or a second ball from a teeing ground, he must do so after his opponent or fellow–competitor has played his first stroke (*Provisional Ball*).

- *Best-Ball and Four-Ball Match Play*
- *Four-Ball Stroke Play*
- *Threesomes and Foursomes*

Order of Play—Match Play (Rule 10–1)

- <u>When Starting Play of Hole</u>: The side that has the honor at the first teeing ground is determined by the order of the draw. In the absence of a draw, the honor should be decided by lot. The side that wins a hole takes the honor at the next teeing ground. If a hole has been halved, the side that had the honor at the previous teeing ground retains it.

- <u>During Play of Hole</u>: After both players have started play of the hole, the ball farther from the hole is played first. If the balls are equidistant from the hole or their positions relative to the hole are not determinable, the ball to be played first should be decided by lot. <u>Note</u>: When the original ball is not to be played as it lies and the player is required to play a ball as nearly as possible at the spot from which the original ball was last played, the order of play is determined by the spot from which the previous stroke was made. When a ball may be played from a spot other than where the previous stroke was made, the order of play is determined by the position where the original ball came to rest.

- <u>Playing Out of Turn</u>: If a player plays when his opponent should have played, there is no penalty, but the opponent may immediately require the player to cancel the stroke so made and, in correct order, play a ball as nearly as possible at the spot from which the original ball was last played.

Order of Play—Stroke Play (Rule 10–2)

- <u>When Starting Play of Hole</u>: The competitor who has the honor at the first teeing ground is determined by the order of the draw. In the absence of a draw, the honor should be decided by lot. The competitor with the lowest score at a hole takes the honor at the next teeing ground. The competitor with the second lowest score plays next and so on. If two or more competitors have the same score at a hole, they play from the next teeing ground in the same order as at the previous teeing ground.

- <u>During Play of Hole</u>: After the competitors have started play of the hole, the ball farthest from the hole is played first. If two or more balls are equidistant from the hole or their positions relative to the hole are not determinable, the ball to be played first should be decided by lot. <u>Note</u>: When the original ball is not to be played as it lies and the player is required to play a ball as nearly as possible at the spot from which the original ball was last played, the order of play is determined by the spot from which the previous stroke was made. When a ball may be played from a spot other than where the previous stroke was made, the order of play is determined by the position where the original ball came to rest.

- <u>Playing Out of Turn</u>: If a competitor plays out of turn, there is no penalty and the ball is played as it lies. If, however, the Committee determines that competitors have agreed to play out of turn to give one of them an advantage, they are disqualified.

Original ball

- *Ball Unfit for Play* (Original ball must be replaced)
- *Procedure When Play Resumed* (Original ball must be placed on the spot from which it was lifted)
- *Provisional Ball* (original ball is lost; lost in water hazard)

Other Conduct Incompatible with Amateurism

- <u>Conduct Detrimental to Amateurism</u>: An amateur golfer must not act in a manner that is detrimental to the best interests of the amateur game.

- <u>Conduct Contrary to the Purpose and Spirit of the Rules</u>: An amateur golfer must not take any action, including actions relating to golf gambling, that is contrary to the purpose and spirit of the Rules.

- *Amateur Status*
- *Gambling*

Out of Bounds

- <u>Definition</u>: *Out of bounds* is beyond the boundaries of the course or any part of the course so marked by the Committee.

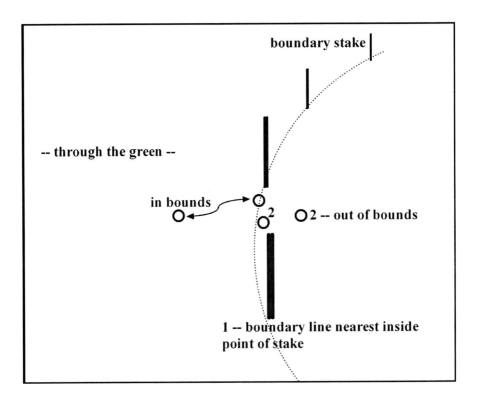

- <u>Inside point of stakes or fence line</u>: When out of bounds is defined by reference to stakes or a fence or as being beyond stakes or a fence, the out of bounds line is determined by the [1—**nearest inside points of the stakes or fence posts**] at ground level excluding angled supports.

- <u>Markers are not obstructions</u>: Objects defining out of bounds such as walls, fences, stakes and railings, are not obstructions and are deemed to be fixed.

- <u>Line is out of bounds</u>: When out of bounds is defined by a line on the ground, the line itself is out of bounds.

- <u>Plane extends vertically up and down</u>: The out of bounds line extends vertically upward and downward.

- <u>All the ball has to lie beyond the boundary</u>: [2—**A ball is out of bounds when all of it lies out of bounds**].

- <u>Can stand out of bounds to play ball</u>: A player may stand out of bounds to play a ball lying within bounds.

- *Ball Lost or Out of Bounds*
- *Ball Played Within Water Hazard*
- *Committee*
- *Improving Lie, Area of Intended Stance or Swing, or Line of Play*
- *Provisional Ball*

Out of shape ball

- *Ball Unfit for Play*

Out of turn

- *Order of Play*
- *Playing out of turn*
- *Second ball*

Outside Agency

- <u>Examples</u>: Fellow player, spectator, animal.

- <u>Definition</u>: An *outside agency* is any agency not part of the match or, in stroke play, not part of the competitor's side, and includes a referee, a marker, an observer and a forecaddie. Neither wind nor water is an outside agency.

- <u>Ball in motion</u>: When a ball in motion is accidentally deflected or stopped by an outside agency, this is a *rub of the green*.

- *By Another Ball*
- *By Outside Agency* (ball at rest moved)

Outside Teeing Ground

- *Playing from Outside Teeing Ground*
- *Tee Box*
- *Teeing*

Outside the impact area

- *Club Face*

Overall result

- *Committee*

Overhanging Hole

- *Ball Overhanging Hole*

P

Pace of Play

- *Be Ready to Play*
- *Lost Ball*
- *Play at Good Pace and Keep Up*
- *Playing Through*
- *Undue Delay; Slow Play*

Paint on ball is damaged

- *Ball Unfit for Play*

Pairings

- *Committee*

Par Competitions

- *Bogey and Par Competitions*
- *Stableford Competitions*

Part of the ball is visible

- *Searching for Ball*

Partner (s)

- <u>Definition</u>: A *partner* is a player associated with another player on the same side. In a threesome, foursome, best–ball or four–ball match, where the context so admits, the word *player* includes his partner or partners.

- *Advice*
- *Best-Ball and Four-Ball Match Play*
- *Clubs*
- *Four-Ball Stroke Play* (Partners need not be present)
- *Maximum of 14 Clubs* (Partners may share clubs)

Parts (clubs)

- *Clubhead*
- *Clubs*

Part-time basis

- *Use of Golf Skill or Reputation*

Payment

- *Instruction*
- *Use of Golf Skill or Reputation*

Pebbles

- *Loose Impediments*

Penalties

- *Disputes and Decisions*

Penalties for Breach of Etiquette

Etiquette

- <u>Disciplinary action</u>: If a player consistently disregards these guidelines during a round or over a period of time to the detriment of others, it is recommended that the Committee consider taking appropriate disciplinary action against the offending player. Such action may, for example, include prohibiting play for a limited time on the course or in a certain number of competitions. This is considered to be justifiable in terms of protecting the interest of the majority of golfers who wish to play in accordance with these guidelines.

- <u>Disqualification</u>: In the case of a serious breach of Etiquette, the Committee may disqualify a player under Rule *Disqualification Penalty; Committee Discretion*.

Penalty disregarded

- *Provisional Ball*

Penalty for Breach of Rule

- *Agreement to Waive Rules*
- *Clubs*
- *Disqualification*
- *Match Play*
- *Maximum of 14 Clubs*
- *Practice*
- *Undue delay*
- *Wrong information*

Penalty Stroke

- <u>Definition</u>: A *penalty stroke* is one added to the score of a player or side under certain Rules. In a threesome or foursome, penalty strokes do not affect the order of play.

Period of play

- *Committee*

Period of waiting

- *Reinstatement of Amateur Status*

Permission to lift ball

- *Lifting Ball When Play Discontinued*

Permit practice

- *Committee*
- *Practice Before or Between Rounds*

Personal Appearance

- *Use of Golf Skill or Reputation*

Personal benefit

- *Use of Golf Skill or Reputation*

Physical assistance

- *Assistance* (Striking the Ball)

Pieces (ball)

- *Unfit for Play*

Pitch-mark

- *Embedded Ball*

Place a ball

- *Ball Lost in Obstruction*

Place the club in front of the ball

- *Touching Line of Putt*

Placed

- *When Ball Dropped or Placed is in Play*

Placement of rakes

- *Rakes*

Placing and Replacing (Rule 20–3)

- <u>By Whom and Where</u>: A ball to be placed under the Rules must be placed by the player or his partner. If a ball is to be replaced, the player, his partner or the person who lifted or moved it must place it on the spot from which it was lifted or moved. In any such case, the player is responsible for any breach of the Rules.

- <u>Ball or marker accidentally moved</u>: If a ball or ball–marker is accidentally moved in the process of placing or replacing the ball, the ball or ball–marker must be replaced. There is no penalty provided the movement of the ball or ball–marker is directly attributable to the specific act of placing or replacing the ball or removing the ball–marker. Otherwise, the player incurs a penalty stroke under Rule *By Player, Partner, Caddie or Equipment* or *Lifting and Marking*.

- <u>Lie of Ball to Be Placed or Replaced Altered</u>: If the original lie of a ball to be placed or replaced has been altered:
  (i) except in a hazard, the ball must be placed in the nearest lie most similar to the original lie that is not more than one club-length from the original lie, not nearer the hole and not in a hazard;
  (ii) in a water hazard, the ball must be placed in accordance with Clause (i) above, except that the ball must be placed in the water hazard;
  (iii) in a bunker, the original lie must be re-created as nearly as possible and the ball must be placed in that lie.

- <u>Spot Not Determinable</u>: If it is impossible to determine the spot where the ball is to be placed or replaced:
  (i) through the green, the ball must be dropped as near as possible to the place where it lay but not in a hazard or on a putting green;
  (ii) in a hazard, the ball must be dropped in the hazard as near as possible to the place where it lay;
  (iii) on the putting green, the ball must be placed as near as possible to the place where it lay but not in a hazard.
  Exception: When resuming play (Rule *Discontinuance of Play; Resumption of Play*), if the spot where the ball is to be placed is impossible to determine, it must be estimated and the ball placed on the estimated spot.

- <u>Ball Fails to Come to Rest on Spot</u>: If a ball when placed fails to come to rest on the spot on which it was placed, there is no penalty and the ball must be replaced. If it still fails to come to rest on that spot:

(i) except in a hazard, it must be placed at the nearest spot where it can be placed at rest that is not nearer the hole and not in a hazard; (ii) in a hazard, it must be placed in the hazard at the nearest spot where it can be placed at rest that is not nearer the hole.

- <u>Ball moves after placed</u>: If a ball when placed comes to rest on the spot on which it is placed, and it subsequently moves, there is no penalty and the ball must be played as it lies, unless the provisions of any other Rule apply.

- <u>Penalty for Breach of Rule</u>: *Match play*, Loss of hole; *Stroke play*, Two strokes.

- *By Player, Partner, Caddie or Equipment* (Ball at Rest Moved)
- *Improving lie, swing, or line of play*
- *Lifting the Ball, Dropping, and Placing*

Plain in Shape

- *Clubhead*

Plates

- *Clubhead*

Play a provisional ball

- *Provisional Ball*

Play alternately

- *Threesomes and Foursomes*

Play at Good Pace and Keep Up

Etiquette

- Players should play at a good pace. The Committee may establish pace of play guidelines that all players should follow. It is a group's responsibility to keep up with the group in front. If it loses a clear hole and it is delaying the group behind, it should invite the group behind to play through, irrespective of the number of players in that group.

Play discontinued

- *Committee*
- *Discontinuance of Play; Resumption of Play*

Play first

- *Order of Play*

Play not conforming to Rules

- *Disputes and Decisions*

Play out of order

- *Threesomes and Foursomes*

Play provisional before search for original ball

- *Provisional Ball*

Play resumed

- *Committee*
- *Discontinuance of Play; Resumption of Play*
- *Procedure When Play Resumed*

Play suspended

- *Committee*
- *Procedure When Play Suspended by Committee*

Play the ball as it lies

- The ball must be played as it lies, unless it can be moved in a specific situation covered by the rules.

Play the same ball

- *Mark the ball*

Play two balls

- *Doubt as to Procedure* (stroke play)

Played as It Lies

- *Ball Played as It Lies*

Played first

- *Order of Play—Match Play*

Played Within Water Hazard

- *Ball Played Within Water Hazard*

Player

- *The Player*

Player gives wrong information

- *Information as to Strokes Taken*

Player moves tee-marker

- *Tee-Markers*

Player waives his right to any prize money

- *Professionalism*

Players appeal to Committee

- *Disputes and Decisions*

Players may practice

- *Committee*

Players of National Prominence

- *Reinstatement of Amateur Status*

Playing Characteristics Changed (Rule 4–2a)

- <u>Club cannot be adjusted</u>: During a stipulated round, the playing characteristics of a club must not be purposely changed by adjustment or by any other means.

- <u>Penalty for Breach of Rule</u>: Disqualification

- *Clubs*
- *Foreign Material* (ball)

Playing for Prize Money

- *Gambling*
- *Prizes*

Playing from Outside Teeing Ground (Rule 11–4)

- <u>Match Play</u>: If a player, when starting a hole, plays a ball from outside the teeing ground there is no penalty, but the opponent may immediately require the player to cancel the stroke and play a ball from within the teeing ground.

- <u>Stroke Play</u>: If a competitor, when starting a hole, plays a ball from outside the teeing ground, he incurs a penalty of two strokes and must then play a ball from within the teeing ground. If the competitor plays a stroke from the next teeing ground without first correcting his mistake or, in the case of the last hole of the round, leaves the putting green without first declaring his intention to correct his mistake, he is DISQUALIFIED. The stroke from outside the teeing ground and any subsequent strokes by the competitor on the hole prior to his correction of the mistake do not count in his score.

- <u>Playing from Wrong Teeing Ground</u>: The above provisions apply.

- *Teeing Ground*

Playing from Wrong Place (Rule 20–7)

- A player has played from a wrong place if he makes a stroke with his ball in play:

  (i) on a part of the course where the Rules do not permit a stroke to be played or a ball to be dropped or placed; or

  (ii) when the Rules require a dropped ball to be re-dropped or a moved ball to be replaced.

  (iii) <u>Playing from Wrong Teeing ground</u>: (Rule 11–5) For a ball played from outside the teeing ground or from a wrong teeing ground, see *Playing from Outside Teeing Ground.*

Penalty

- <u>Match Play</u>: If a player makes a stroke from a wrong place, he loses the hole.

- <u>Stroke Play</u>: If a competitor makes a stroke from a wrong place, he incurs a penalty of two strokes under the applicable Rule. He must play out the hole with the ball played from the wrong place, without correcting his error, provided he has not committed a *serious breach*. If a competitor becomes aware that he has played from a wrong place and believes that he may have committed a serious breach, he must, before making a stroke on the next teeing ground, play out the hole with a second ball dropped or placed in accordance with the Rules. If the hole being played is the last hole of the round, he must declare, before leaving the putting green, that he will play out the hole with a second ball dropped or placed in accordance with the Rules.

- <u>Disqualification</u>: The competitor must report the facts to the Committee before returning his Scorecard; if he fails to do so, he is disqualified. The Committee must determine whether the competitor has committed a *serious breach* of the applicable Rule. If he has, the score with the second ball counts and the competitor must add two penalty strokes to his score with that ball. If the competitor has committed a serious breach and has failed to correct it as outlined above, he is *disqualified.*

- <u>Serious Breach</u>: A competitor is deemed to have committed a serious breach of the applicable Rule if the Committee considers he has gained a significant advantage as a result of playing from a wrong place.

- <u>Strokes that are disregarded</u>: If a competitor plays a second ball under this Rule and it is ruled not to count, strokes made with that ball and penalty strokes incurred solely by playing that ball are disregarded. If the second ball is ruled to count, the stroke made from the wrong place and any strokes subsequently taken with the original ball including penalty strokes incurred solely by playing that ball are disregarded.

- *Lifting the Ball, Dropping, and Placing*

Playing Moving Ball (Rule 14–5)

- <u>No stroke while moving</u>: A player must not make a stroke at his ball while it is moving.

- <u>Exceptions</u>: (1) Ball falling off tee; (2) Striking the ball more than once; (3) Ball moving in water.

- <u>Ball moves after stroke begun</u>: When the ball begins to move only after the player has begun the stroke or the backward movement of his club for the stroke, he incurs no penalty under this Rule for playing a moving ball, but he is not exempt from any penalty under the following Rules: (1) Ball at rest moved by player; (2) Ball at rest moving after address; (3) Ball purposely deflected or stopped by player, partner or caddie.

- *Striking the Ball*

Playing out of turn

- <u>Match Play</u>: If you play at your opponent's turn, there's no penalty; however, your opponent can make you cancel the stroke and take it again in the right order, placing the ball exactly where it had been.

- <u>Stroke Play</u>: There's no penalty for playing out of turn in stroke play; the ball played as it lies. However, if competitors agree to play in an order differing from the honor system for the purpose of giving someone an advantage, they will be DISQUALIFIED.

- *Order of Play—Match Play*
- *Order of Play—Stroke Play*
- *Second ball*

Playing outside the teeing ground

- You are supposed to start the hole by playing a ball from inside the teeing ground; otherwise, there are the following penalties:

- <u>Match Play</u>: Your opponent can make you cancel the stroke and play again from within the area.

- <u>Stroke Play</u>: You're penalized two strokes and must take the stroke again from within the area. Any strokes taken outside the teeing ground won't count in your score.

- <u>Disqualification</u>: If you reach the next teeing ground and make a stroke without having replayed the previous stroke—or on the last hole, leave the putting green without stating your intention to correct it—you'll be DISQUALIFIED.

- *Teeing Ground*

Playing the proper ball

- *Ball*

Playing Through

- When a group falls one clear hole behind the group ahead.

- When the group ahead is searching for a ball.

- *Pace of Play*

Point out a line for putting

- *Advice*
- *Putting Line*

Points

- *Stableford Competitions*

Points Not Covered by Rules (Rule 1–4)

- If any point in dispute is not covered by the Rules, the decision should be made in accordance with equity.

- *Game*

Points total

- *Committee*

Position of rakes

- *Rakes*

Position of the hole

- *Flagstick Attended, Removed or Held Up*

Position or lie of the ball

- *Exerting Influence on Ball* (movement of a ball)
- *Improving Lie, Area of Intended Stance or Swing, or Line of Play*
- *Lifting and Cleaning Ball*
- *Lifting Ball When Play Discontinued*

Post

- Out–of–bounds marked by INSIDE point of post.

Powder

- *Artificial Devices and Unusual Equipment*

Power (Committee)

- *Committee*

Practice (Rule 7)

Before or Between Rounds (Rule 7–1)

- <u>Match Play</u>: On any day of a match–play competition, a player may practice on the competition course before a round.

- <u>Stroke Play</u>: Before a round or play–off on any day of a stroke–play competition, a competitor must not practice on the competition course or test the surface of any putting green on the course by rolling a ball or roughening or scraping the surface. When two or more rounds of a stroke–play competition are to be played over consecutive days, a competitor must not practice between those rounds on any competition course remaining to be played, or test the surface of any putting green on such course by rolling a ball or roughening or scraping the surface. <u>Exception</u>: Practice putting or chipping on or near the first teeing ground before starting a round or play–off is permitted.

- Penalty for Breach of Rule is DISQUALIFICATION.

- <u>Note</u>: The Committee may, in the conditions of a competition (Rule *Conditions; Waiving Rule*), prohibit practice on the competition course on any day of a match–play competition or permit practice on the competition course or part of the course (Rule *The Course*) on any day of or between rounds of a stroke–play competition.

- *Committee*
- *Four-Ball Stroke Play*
- *Bogey and Par Competitions*
- *Stableford Competitions*

During Round (Rule 7–2)

- <u>Not during play of hole</u>: A player must not make a practice stroke during play of a hole. A practice swing is not a practice stroke and may be taken at any place, provided the player does not breach the Rules.

- <u>Between play of two holes</u>: Between the play of two holes, a player must not make a practice stroke, except that he may practice putting or chipping on or near: (a) the putting green of the hole last played; (b) any practice putting green; or (c) the teeing ground of the next hole to be played in the round; provided a practice stroke is not made from a hazard and does not unduly delay play.

- <u>Continuing play of hole</u>: Strokes made in continuing the play of a hole, the result of which has been decided, are not practice strokes. <u>Exception</u>: When play has been suspended by the Committee, a player may, prior to resumption of play, practice (a) as provided in this Rule, (b) anywhere other than on the competition course and (c) as otherwise permitted by the Committee.

- <u>Penalty for breach of rule</u>: *Match Play*, Loss of hole; *Stroke Play*, Two strokes. In the event of a breach between the play of two holes, the penalty applies to the next hole.

- <u>Committee may prohibit</u>: The Committee may, in the conditions of a competition, prohibit: (a) practice on or near the putting green of the hole last played; and (b) rolling a ball on the putting green of the hole last played.

- *Committee* (practice ground)

Practice session

- *Expenses*

Preferred lies

- *Course Record*

Present

- *Best-Ball and Four-Ball Match Play*

Present case

- *Procedure for Enforcement of the Rules*

Press anything down

- *Touching Line of Putt*

Pressed on the ground (club)

- *Improving Lie, Area of Intended Stance or Swing, or Line of Play*

Prevent falling

- *Ball in Hazard*

Preventing Unnecessary Damage

Etiquette

- Divots: Players should avoid causing damage to the course by removing divots when taking practice swings or by hitting the head of a club into the ground, whether in anger or for any other reason.

- Putting green: Players should ensure that no damage is done to the putting green when putting down bags or the flagstick. Players should not lean on their clubs when on the putting green, particularly when removing the ball from the hole.

- Hole: In order to avoid damaging the hole, players and caddies should not stand too close to the hole and should take care during the handling of the flagstick and the removal of a ball from the hole. The head of a club should not be used to remove a ball from the hole.

- Flagstick: The flagstick should be properly replaced in the hole before players leave the putting green.

- Golf carts: Local notices regulating the movement of golf carts should be strictly observed.

Primary occupation

- *Use of Golf Skill or Reputation*

Prior to Round

- *Damaged Clubs*

Priority on the Course

- <u>Etiquette</u>: Unless otherwise determined by the Committee, priority on the course is determined by a group's pace of play. Any group playing a whole round is entitled to pass a group playing a shorter round.

- *Playing Through*

Privileges at a golf course

- *Use of Golf Skill or Reputation*

Prizes

Amateur Status

- <u>Playing for Prize Money</u>: An amateur golfer must not play golf for prize money or its equivalent in a match, tournament or exhibition. A player may participate in an event in which prize money or its equivalent is offered, provided that prior to participation he irrevocably waives his right to accept prize money in that event. (See *USGA Policy on Gambling* for explanation of playing for prize money.)

- <u>Prize Limits</u>: An amateur golfer must not:

  a. Accept a prize (including all prizes received in any one tournament or exhibition for any event, or series of events, in which golf skill is a factor) of a retail value greater than $750 (except for symbolic prizes); <u>Exception</u>, Hole-In-One Prizes: The limit applies to a prize for a hole-in-one. However, such a prize may be accepted in addition to any other prize won in the same competition.

b. Accept a prize of money or the equivalent of money;

c. Convert a prize into money;

d. Accept expenses in any amount to a golf competition (except as provided in Rule *Expenses*); or

e. Because of golf skill or reputation, accept in connection with any golfing event:

(i) money, or

(ii) anything else, other than merchandise of nominal value provided to all players.

- <u>Testimonial Awards</u>: An amateur golfer must not accept a testimonial award of a retail value greater than $750. <u>Multiple Awards</u>: An amateur golfer may accept more than one testimonial award from different donors, even if their total retail value exceeds $750, provided they are not presented so as to evade the limit for a single award.

- *Amateur Status*
- *Gambling*
- *Reinstatement of Amateur Status*
- *Professionalism*

Probing for ball

- *Searching for Ball*

Procedure for Applications

- *Reinstatement of Amateur Status*

Procedure for Enforcement of the Rules

Amateur Status

- <u>Decision on a Breach</u>: If a possible breach of the Rules by a person claiming to be an amateur golfer comes to the attention of the Committee, it is a matter for the Committee to decide whether a breach has occurred. Each case will be investigated to the extent deemed appropriate by the Committee and considered on its merits. The decision of the Committee is final, subject to an appeal as provided in these Rules.

- <u>Enforcement</u>: Upon a decision that a person has breached the Rules, the Committee may declare the Amateur Status of the person forfeited or require the person to refrain or desist from specified actions as a condition of retaining his Amateur Status. The Committee should notify the person and may notify any interested golf association of any action taken under this Rule.

- <u>Appeals Procedure</u>: Any person who considers that any action he is proposing to take might endanger his Amateur Status may submit particulars to the staff of the USGA for an advisory opinion. If dissatisfied with the staff's advisory opinion, he may, by written notice to the staff within 30 days after being notified of the advisory opinion, appeal to the Committee, in which case he must be given reasonable notice of the Committee's next meeting at which the matter may be heard and must be entitled to present his case in person or in writing. In such cases the staff must submit to the Committee all information provided by the player together with staff's findings and recommendation, and the Committee must issue a decision on the matter. If dissatisfied with the Committee's decision, the player may, by written notice to the staff within 30 days after being notified of the decision, appeal to the Executive Committee, in which case he must be given reasonable notice of the next meeting of the Executive Committee at which the matter may be heard and must be entitled to present his case in person or in writing. The decision of the Executive Committee is final.

- *Amateur Status*
- *Committee Decision*
- *Reinstatement of Amateur Status*

Procedure When Play Resumed (Rule 6–8d)

- <u>Resumed where discontinued</u>: Play must be resumed from where it was discontinued, even if resumption occurs on a subsequent day. The player must, either before or when play is resumed, proceed as follows:

  (i) <u>Original ball replaced to original spot</u>: If the player has lifted the ball, he must, provided he was entitled to lift it, place a ball on the spot from which the original ball was lifted. Otherwise, the original ball must be placed on the spot from which it was lifted;

  (ii) <u>Lift, clean, replace</u>: If the player entitled to lift his ball has not done so, he may lift, clean and replace the ball, or substitute a ball on the spot from which the original ball was lifted. Before lifting the ball he must mark its position; or

  (iii) <u>Ball-marker moved</u>: If the player's ball or ball-marker is moved (including by wind or water) while play is discontinued, a ball or ball-marker must be placed on the spot from which the original ball or ball-marker was moved. If the spot where the ball is to be placed is impossible to determine, it must be estimated and the ball placed on the estimated spot.

- <u>Penalty for breach of rule</u>: *Match Play*, Loss of hole; *Stroke Play*, Two strokes.

- *Discontinuance of Play*
- *The Player*

Procedure When Play Suspended by Committee (Rule 6–8b)

- <u>Between two holes</u>: When play is suspended by the Committee, if the players in a match or group are between the play of two holes, they must not resume play until the Committee has ordered a resumption of play.

- <u>Stop or finish hole</u>: If they have started play of a hole, they may discontinue play immediately or continue play of the hole, provided they do so without delay. If the players choose to continue play of the hole, they are permitted to discontinue play before completing it. In any case, play must be discontinued after the hole is completed.

- <u>Resume when Committee orders</u>: The players must resume play when the Committee has ordered a resumption of play.

- <u>Dangerous situations</u>: The Committee may rule that, in potentially dangerous situations, play must be discontinued immediately following a suspension of play by the Committee. If a player fails to discontinue play immediately, he is disqualified unless circumstances warrant waiving the penalty.

- <u>Penalty for breach of rule</u>: DISQUALIFICATION.

- *Discontinuance of Play*
- *The Player*

Professional agent or sponsor

- *Expenses*
- *Professionalism*

Professional golfer

- *Professionalism*

Professional Golfers Organization

- *Professionalism*

Professional tour

- *Professionalism*

Professionalism

- Amateur golfer must not: An *amateur golfer* must not take any action for the purpose of becoming a professional golfer and must not identify himself as a professional golfer. Such actions include:

  - applying for a professional's position;

  - directly or indirectly receiving services or payment from a professional agent or sponsor, commercial or otherwise;

  - directly or indirectly entering into a written or oral agreement with a professional agent or sponsor, commercial or otherwise;

  - agreeing to accept payment or compensation for allowing one's name or likeness as a player of golf skill or reputation to be used for any commercial purpose.

- Exception 1: Applying unsuccessfully for the position of assistant professional.

- Exception 2: Entering and playing in any stage of a competition to qualify for a professional tour, provided the player first waives his right to any prize money.

- <u>Professional Golfers Organization</u>: An amateur golfer must not apply for or receive benefit from membership in any organization of professional golfers.

- *Amateur Status*
- *Reinstatement of Amateur Status*

Prohibit

- *Ball in Hazard*
- *Caddie*
- *Practice Before or Between Rounds*
- *Relief for Ball in Water Hazard*

Promote

- *Use of Golf Skill or Reputation*

Promotion

- *Expenses*

Protection from the elements

- *Assistance* (Striking the Ball)
- *Striking the ball*

Provide Scorecards

- *Committee*

Provisional Ball (Rule 27–2)

- <u>Definition</u>: A *provisional ball* is a ball played under this Rule that may be lost outside a water hazard or may be out of bounds.

- After 5–minute search and stroke is taken, original ball is *lost* and provisional ball is in play.

Procedure

- <u>Play before search for original ball</u>: If a ball may be lost outside a water hazard or may be out of bounds, to save time the player may play another ball provisionally in accordance with Rule *Ball Lost or Out of Bounds*. The player must inform his opponent in match play or his marker or a fellow–competitor in stroke play that he intends to play a provisional ball, and he must play it before he or his partner goes forward to search for the original ball.

- <u>Stroke and distance</u>: If he fails to do so and plays another ball, that ball is not a provisional ball and becomes the ball in play under penalty of stroke and distance (Rule *Ball Lost or Out of Bounds*); the original ball is lost.

- <u>Second provisional ball</u>: If a provisional ball played under this Rule might be lost outside a water hazard or out of bounds, the player may play another provisional ball. If another provisional ball is played, it bears the same relationship to the previous provisional ball as the first provisional ball bears to the original.

When Provisional Ball Becomes Ball in Play

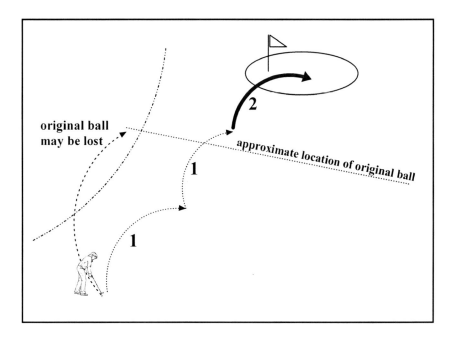

- <u>Hit provisional ball up to original ball</u>: The player may play a provisional ball [1—until he reaches the place where the original ball is likely to be]. If he [2—makes a stroke with the provisional ball from the place where the original ball is likely to be or from a point nearer the hole than that place], the original ball is lost and the provisional ball becomes the ball in play under penalty of stroke and distance (Rule *Ball Lost or Out of Bounds*).

- <u>Original ball lost or out of bounds, provisional in play</u>: If the original ball is lost outside a water hazard or is out of bounds, the provisional ball becomes the ball in play, under penalty of stroke and distance (Rule *Ball Lost or Out of Bounds*).

- <u>Original ball lost in water hazard</u>: If there is reasonable evidence that the original ball is lost in a water hazard, the player must proceed in accordance with Rule *Relief for Ball in Water Hazard*.

- Obstruction or abnormal ground condition: If there is reasonable evidence that the original ball is lost in an obstruction (Rule *Ball Lost in Obstruction*) or an abnormal ground condition (Rule *Abnormal Ground Conditions*) the player may proceed under the applicable Rule.

When Provisional Ball to Be Abandoned

- Original ball neither lost nor out of bounds: If the original ball is neither lost nor out of bounds, the player must abandon the provisional ball and continue playing the original ball. If he makes any further strokes at the provisional ball, he is playing a wrong ball and the provisions of Rule *Wrong Ball* apply.

- Abandoned provisional ball stroke and penalty disregarded: If a player plays a provisional ball under the procedure above, the strokes made after this Rule has been invoked with a provisional ball abandoned and penalty strokes incurred solely by playing that ball are disregarded.

- *Ball Lost or Out of Bounds*

Puddle (on green)

- *Abnormal Ground Conditions* (diagram)

Punch marks

- *Club Face*

Purpose and Spirit of the Rules

- *Other Conduct Incompatible with Amateurism*

Purposely deflected or stopped (ball)

- *By Outside Agency*

Push the ball

- *Striking the Ball*

Putt

- *Abnormal Ground Conditions*

Putter

- *Club Face*
- *Clubhead*
- *Clubs*
- *Grip*
- *Shaft*

Putting

- *Practice*
- *Putting Line*

Putting Green (Rule 16)

- <u>Definition</u>: The *putting green* is all ground of the hole being played that is specially prepared for putting or otherwise defined as such by the Committee. A ball is on the putting green when any part of it touches the putting green.

- *Ball Lost in Obstruction*
- *Ball Overhanging Hole*

- *Improving lie, swing, or line of play*
- *Lifting and Cleaning Ball*
- *Making Stroke While Another Ball in Motion*
- *Putting Line*
- *Repair of Hole Plugs, Ball Marks and Other Damage*
- *Standing Astride or on Line of Putt*
- *Testing*
- *Touching Line of Putt*
- *Wrong Putting Green*

Putting Line

- *Indicating Line of Play*

Putting surface

- *Practice*

Q

Qualify for a professional tour

- *Professionalism*

Qualifying

- *Disputes and Decisions*

R

Raise the ball off the ground

- *Teeing*

Raised lips

- *Club Face*

Raised rib

- *Grip*

Rake Sand Traps

- After every shot in a trap.

Rakes

- <u>Outside bunkers</u>: (Misc./2) It is recommended that rakes should be left outside bunkers in areas where they are least likely to affect the movement of the ball. Ultimately, it is a matter for the Committee to decide where it wishes rakes to be placed.

Reasonable evidence

- *Relief for Ball in Water Hazard*

Reasonable expenses

- *Expenses*

Receive reimbursement

- *Expenses*

Receive strokes (handicap)

- *Committee*

Receiving services or payment from a professional agent or sponsor

- *Professionalism*

Record handicap

- *Committee*
- *Disputes and Decisions*
- *Handicap*

Record score

- *Course Record*

Recording Scores

- *Stroke Play*

Recover ball

- *Searching for Ball*

Red stakes or lines

- Defines boundary of a LATERAL WATER HAZARD.

- Stakes and lines are part of the hazard.

- *Water Hazards*

Re-dropping ball

- *Dropping and Re-Dropping*

Referee

- <u>Definition</u>: A *referee* is one who is appointed by the Committee to accompany players to decide questions of fact and apply the Rules. He must act on any breach of a Rule that he observes or is reported to him. A referee should not attend the flagstick, stand at or mark the position of the hole, or lift the ball or mark its position.

- *Committee* (Referee's duties)
- *Disputes and Decisions*

Referred to the Committee

- *Disputes and Decisions*

Referred to USGA

- *Disputes and Decisions*

Refusal to Comply with a Rule (stroke play)
(Rule 3–4)

- <u>Disqualification</u>: If a competitor refuses to comply with a Rule affecting the rights of another competitor, he is DISQUALIFIED.

- *Bogey and Par Competitions*
- *Four-Ball Stroke Play*
- *Stableford Competitions*
- *Stroke Play*

Regional golf association

- *Expenses*

Reimbursement

- *Expenses*

Reinstatement of Amateur Status

General

- <u>Committee sole authority</u>: The Committee has the sole authority to reinstate a person to Amateur Status, prescribe a waiting period necessary for reinstatement or to deny reinstatement, subject to an appeal as provided in the Rules.

Applications for Reinstatement

Each application for reinstatement will be considered on its merits, with consideration normally being given to the following principles:

- <u>Awaiting Reinstatement</u>: The professional golfer is considered to hold an advantage over the amateur golfer by reason of having devoted himself to the game as his profession; other persons infringing the Rules also obtain advantages not available to the amateur golfer. They do not necessarily lose such advantages merely by deciding to cease infringing the Rules. Therefore, an applicant for reinstatement to Amateur Status must undergo a period awaiting reinstatement as prescribed by the Committee. The period awaiting reinstatement generally starts from the date of the person's last breach of the Rules unless the Committee decides that it starts from either (a) the date when the person's last breach became known to the Committee, or (b) such other date determined by the Committee.

- Period Awaiting Reinstatement:

(i) Professionalism

Generally, the period awaiting reinstatement is related to the period the person was in breach of the Rules. However, no applicant is normally eligible for reinstatement until he has conducted himself in accordance with the Rules for a period of at least one year. It is recommended that the following guidelines on periods awaiting reinstatement be applied by the Committee:

Period of Breach	Period Awaiting Reinstatement
under 5 years	1 year
5 years or more	2 years

However, the period may be extended if the applicant has played extensively for prize money, regardless of performance. In all cases, the Committee reserves the right to extend or to shorten the period awaiting reinstatement.

(ii) Other Breaches of the Rules

A period awaiting reinstatement of one year will normally be required. However, the period may be extended if the breach is considered serious.

- <u>Number of Reinstatements</u>: A person is not normally eligible to be reinstated more than twice.

- <u>Players of National Prominence</u>: A player of national prominence who has been in breach of the Rules for more than five years is not normally eligible for reinstatement.

- <u>Status While Awaiting Reinstatement</u>: An applicant for reinstatement must comply with these Rules, as they apply to an amateur golfer, during his period awaiting reinstatement. An applicant for reinstatement is not eligible to enter competitions as an amateur golfer. However, he may enter competitions and win a prize solely among members of a club where he is a member, subject to the approval of the club. He must not represent such club against other clubs unless with the approval of the clubs in the competition and/or the organizing Committee. An applicant for reinstatement may enter competitions that are not limited to amateur golfers, subject to the conditions of competition, without prejudicing his application, provided he does so as an applicant for reinstatement. He must waive his right to any prize money offered in the competition and must not accept any prize reserved for an amateur golfer (Rule *Prizes*).

Procedure for Applications

- <u>Submitted to Committee</u>: Each application for reinstatement must be submitted to the Committee, in accordance with such procedures as may be laid down and including such information as the Committee may require.

- <u>Appeals Procedure</u>: See *Procedure for Enforcement of the Rules.*

- *Amateur Status*
- *Committee Decision*

Relief

	Through the green	Bunker	Water hazard	Green
Natural objects such as leaves, twigs, rocks	*Loose Impediments*			
Artificial movable objects such as cans, rakes, stakes, and golf carts	*Movable Obstruction*			
Artificial immovable objects such as ball washers, fences, sheds, cart paths	*Immovable Obstruction*			
Abnormal ground conditions such as ground under repair, casual water, dirt holes by burrowing animals	*Abnormal Ground Conditions*			
Declaring a ball unplayable	*Ball Unplayable*			

- *Ball Lost in Obstruction*
- *Searching for Ball*
- *Wrong Putting Green*

Relief for Ball in Water Hazard (Rule 26–1)

- <u>Reasonable evidence</u>: It is a question of fact whether a ball lost after having been struck toward a water hazard is lost inside or outside the hazard. In order to treat the ball as lost in the hazard, there must be reasonable evidence that the ball lodged in it. In the absence of such evidence, the ball must be treated as a lost ball and Rule *Ball Lost or Out of Bounds* applies.

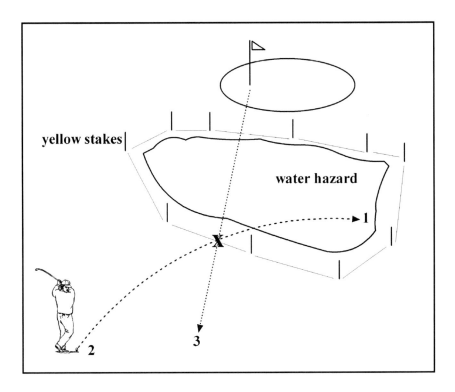

- <u>Ball in or lost in water hazard</u> (yellow stakes): If a [**1—ball is in or is lost in a water hazard**] (whether the ball lies in water or not), the player may under penalty of one stroke:

    a. <u>Play another ball from original spot</u>: Play a ball as nearly as possible at the [**2—spot from which the original ball was last played**] (see Rule *Making Next Stroke from Where Previous Stroke Made*); or,

    b. <u>Drop a ball</u>: [**3—Drop a ball behind the water hazard**], keeping the point at which the original ball last crossed the margin of the water hazard (**X**) directly between the hole and the spot on which the ball is dropped, with no limit to how far behind the water hazard the ball may be dropped; or,

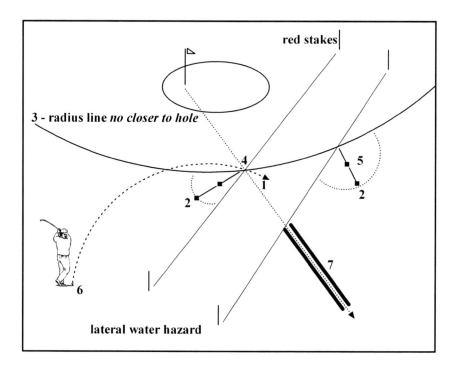

c. <u>Lateral water hazard</u> (red stakes): As additional options available only if the [1—**ball last crossed the margin of a lateral water hazard**], drop a ball outside the water hazard within [2— **two club-lengths**] of and [3—**not nearer the hole**] than:

[4—**the point where the original ball last crossed the margin of the water hazard**]; or,

[5—**a point on the opposite margin of the water hazard equidistant from the hole**].

Play a ball as nearly as possible at the [6—**spot from which the original ball was last played**]

[7—**Drop a ball behind the water hazard**], keeping the point at which the original ball last crossed the margin of the water hazard (4) directly between the hole and the spot on which the ball is dropped, with no limit to how far behind the water hazard the ball may be dropped

- <u>Lift and clean</u>: The ball may be lifted and cleaned when proceeding under this Rule.

- *Ball in Hazard*
- *Ball Lost or Out of Bounds*
- *Ball Moving in Water*
- *Prohibit*
- *Provisional Ball*
- *Water Hazards* (Rule 26)

Removal of a loose impediment

- *Loose Impediments*

Remove flagstick

- *Ball Resting Against Flagstick*

Remove obstruction

- *Ball in Hazard*
- *Ball Lost in Obstruction*
- *By Player, Partner, Caddie or Equipment* (Ball at Rest Moved)
- *Movable Obstruction*
- *Touching Line of Putt*

Removed (flagstick)

- *Flagstick Attended, Removed or Held Up*

Removing a loose impediment

- *By Player, Partner, Caddie or Equipment* (Ball at Rest Moved)

Removing items on or near the ball

- *Improving lie, swing, or line of play*
- *Searching for Ball*

Removing or pressing down

- *Improving Lie, Area of Intended Stance or Swing, or Line of Play*

Repair and Replacement of Damaged Clubs

- *Damaged Clubs*

Repair hole

- *Committee*

Repair of Divots, Ball-Marks and Damage by Shoes

- Etiquette: Players should carefully repair any divot holes made by them and any damage to the putting green made by the impact of a ball (whether or not made by the player himself). On completion of the hole by all players in the group, damage to the putting green caused by golf shoes should be repaired.

Repair of Hole Plugs, Ball Marks and Other Damage (Rule 16–1c)

- Player may repair damage: The player may repair an old hole plug or damage to the putting green caused by the impact of a ball, whether or not the player's ball lies on the putting green (See *Putting Green*).

- <u>Ball or ball-marker is accidentally moved</u>: If a ball or ball–marker is accidentally moved in the process of the repair, the ball or ball–marker must be replaced. There is no penalty provided the movement of the ball is directly attributable to the specific act of repairing an old hole plug or damage to the putting green caused by the impact of a ball. Otherwise, the player incurs a penalty stroke under Rule *Ball at Rest Moved*.

- <u>Other damage must not be repaired</u>: Any other damage to the putting green must not be repaired if it might assist the player in his subsequent play of the hole (See *Improving Lie, Area of Intended Stance or Swing, or Line of Play*).

- *By Player, Partner, Caddie or Equipment* (Ball at Rest Moved)
- *Touching Line of Putt*

Replace divots

- *Improving Lie, Area of Intended Stance or Swing, or Line of Play*

Replace the ball

- *Ball falling off the tee*
- *Placing and Replacing*
- *Searching for Ball*

Representation of Side

- *Best-Ball and Four-Ball Match Play*
- *Four-Ball Stroke Play*

Reputation

- *Use of Golf Skill or Reputation*

Request opinion

- *Disputes and Decisions*

Requirements for the ball

- *Ball*

Rescinded penalty

- *Disputes and Decisions*

Resin

- *Artificial Devices and Unusual Equipment*

Responsibility for playing the proper ball

- *Ball*
- *Identifying Ball*

Rest

- *By Another Ball*

Resting Against Flagstick (ball)

- *Ball Resting Against Flagstick*

Result of each hole

- *Committee*

Results of a professional competition

- *Gambling*

Results officially announced

- *Disputes and Decisions*

Resumption of Play

- *Committee*
- *Discontinuance of Play; Resumption of Play*
- *Placing and Replacing*
- *Procedure When Play Resumed*
- *Procedure When Play Suspended by Committee*

Retail Value

- <u>Amateur Status</u>: The *retail value* of a prize is the price at which it is generally available at the time of the award.

- *Prizes*

Retains honor

- *Order of Play*

Re-teed

- *Ball Falling Off Tee*

Returned a Scorecard

- *Disputes and Decisions*
- *Scoring and Scorecard*
- *Stroke Play*

Rib

- *Grip*

Right order of play

- *Playing out of turn*

Right to prize money

- *Gambling*
- *Professionalism*

Rights of another competitor

- *Refusal to Comply with a Rule* (stroke play)

Rigid

- *Clubhead*

Rocks

- *Loose Impediments*

Rods

- *Clubhead*

Roll of the ball

- *The Ball*

Rolling a ball

- *Abnormal Ground Conditions*
- *Practice Before or Between Rounds*
- *Testing*

Roughening the putting surface

- *Practice Before or Between Rounds*
- *Testing*

Roughness

- *Club Face*

Round played on more than one day

- *Committee*

Rounding of groove edges

- *Club Face*

Rub of the Green

- Definition: A *rub of the green* occurs when a ball in motion is accidentally deflected or stopped by any outside agency (see Rule *By Outside Agency*).

Rule or Rules

- Definition: The term *Rule* includes:

  a. The Rules of Golf and their interpretations as contained in "Decisions on the Rules of Golf";

  b. Any Conditions of Competition established by the Committee under Rule *Conditions; Waiving Rule* and *Local Rules; Conditions of the Competition*;

  c. Any Local Rules established by the Committee under Rule *Local Rules* and *Conditions of the Competition*; and

  d. The specifications on clubs and the ball in *Design* and *The Ball*.

- Amateur Status: The term *Rule* or *Rules* refers to the *Rules of Amateur Status* as determined by the USGA.

- Player and caddie responsible: The player and his caddie are responsible for knowing the Rules. During a stipulated round, for any breach of a Rule by his caddie, the player incurs the applicable penalty. **(Rule 6–1)**

- Rules are ignored: *Match play*, both players are disqualified; *Stroke play*, all the players are disqualified.

- *Committee* (Rule waived)
- *The Player*

Rules of Amateur Status

- *Amateur Status*

Runners

- *Clubhead*

S

Safety

Etiquette

- <u>Don't stand too close</u>: Players should ensure that no one is standing close by or in a position to be hit by the club, the ball or any stones, pebbles, twigs or the like when they make a stroke or practice swing.

- <u>Players out of range</u>: Players should not play until the players in front are out of range.

- <u>Alert greenstaff</u>: Players should always alert greenstaff nearby or ahead when they are about to make a stroke that might endanger them.

- <u>Shout *fore*</u>: If a player plays a ball in a direction where there is a danger of hitting someone, he should immediately shout a warning. The traditional word of warning in such situation is *fore*.

Sale of written golf instruction

- *Instruction*

Same score

- *Order of Play*

Sand & Soil

- Sand and soil is a loose impediment ONLY on the putting green.

- *Improving lie, swing, or line of play*
- *Searching for Ball*

Sand Trap

- *Bunker*

Sandblasting

- *Club Face*

Scholarships

- *Use of Golf Skill or Reputation*

Schools

- *Instruction*

Score

- *Course Record*
- *Scoring and Scorecard*

Scoring and Scorecard

- <u>Etiquette</u>: In stroke play, a player who is acting as a marker should, if necessary, on the way to the next tee, check the score with the player concerned and record it.

- <u>Playing second ball</u>: If during stroke play you get confused about what you're allowed or supposed to do in a certain situation, you're allowed to play a second ball after telling the other players what you're going to do and which ball you will score for that hole. You must tell the Committee what happened before turning in your scorecard, or you will be DISQUALIFIED.

- <u>Marker records</u>: After each hole the marker should check the score with the competitor and record it. On completion of the round the marker must sign the scorecard and hand it to the competitor. If more than one marker records the scores, each must sign for the part for which he is responsible. (**Rule 6–6a**)

- <u>Player checks and signs scorecard</u>: After completion of the round, the competitor should check his score for each hole and settle any doubtful points with the Committee. He must ensure that the marker or markers have signed the Scorecard, sign the Scorecard himself and return it to the Committee as soon as possible. No alteration may be made on a Scorecard after the competitor has returned it to the Committee. (**Rule 6–6b,c**)

- <u>Correctness of score</u>: The competitor is responsible for the correctness of the score recorded for each hole on his Scorecard. If he returns a score for any hole lower than actually taken, he is DISQUALIFIED. If he returns a score for any hole higher than actually taken, the score as returned stands. (**Rule 6–6d**)

- <u>Committee adds scores</u>: The Committee is responsible for the addition of scores and application of the handicap recorded on the Scorecard.

- <u>Penalty for Breach of Rule</u>: DISQUALIFICATION.

- *Bogey and Par Competitions*
- *Committee* (scores cancelled)
- *Disputes and Decisions*
- *Disqualification*
- *Four-Ball Stroke Play*
- *Handicap*

- *Stableford Competitions*
- *The Player*

Scrape the ball

- *Striking the ball*

Scraping the putting surface

- *Practice Before or Between Rounds*
- *Testing*

Scratched

- *Ball Unfit for Play*
- *Damaged Clubs* (clubhead)

Searching for Ball; Seeing Ball (Rule 12–1)

- Five (5) minute limit for search.

- <u>Provisional ball</u>: After a search and a stroke is taken with a provisional ball, the original ball is "lost" and the provisional ball is in play.

- <u>Player may touch or bend long grass</u>: In searching for his ball anywhere on the course, the player may touch or bend long grass, rushes, bushes, whins, heather or the like, but only to the extent necessary to find and identify it, provided that this does not improve the lie of the ball, the area of his intended stance or swing or his line of play.

- <u>Not necessarily entitled to see the ball</u>: A player is not necessarily entitled to see his ball when making a stroke. In a hazard, if a ball is believed to be covered by loose impediments or sand, the player may remove by probing or raking with a club or otherwise, as many loose impediments or as much sand as will enable him to see a part of the ball. If an excess is removed, there is no penalty and the ball must be re–covered so that only a part of the ball is visible. If the ball is moved during the removal, there is no penalty; the ball must be replaced and, if necessary, re–covered.

- <u>Ball accidentally moved during search</u>: If a ball lying in an abnormal ground condition is accidentally moved during search, there is no penalty; the ball must be replaced, unless the player elects to take relief under *Abnormal Ground Conditions*. There is no penalty for causing the ball to move provided the movement of the ball was directly attributable to the specific act of probing.

- <u>Ball lying in water</u>: If a ball is believed to be lying in water in a water hazard, the player may probe for it with a club or otherwise. If the ball is moved in probing, it must be replaced, unless the player elects to take relief under *Abnormal Ground Conditions*.

- <u>Penalty for Breach of Rule</u>: *Match Play*, Loss of hole; *Stroke Play*, Two strokes.

- *Abnormal Ground Conditions*
- *By Opponent, Caddie or Equipment in Match Play* (ball at rest moved)
- *Identifying Bal*
- *Loose Impediments*
- *Lost Ball*
- *Provisional Ball*

Second ball

- <u>Play second if get confused</u>: If during stroke play you get confused about what you're allowed or supposed to do in a certain situation, you're allowed to play a second ball after telling the other players what you're going to do and which ball you will score for that hole. You must tell the Committee what happened before turning in your scorecard, or you will be DISQUALIFIED. If what you decided to do after you were confused turned out to be the legal course to take, then the second ball will be your score.

- <u>From teeing ground</u>: If you play a provisional or second ball from the teeing ground, you must wait until your opponent or fellow–competitor has played his first stroke. If you don't wait, you're out of turn (see *Order of Play—Provisional Ball or Second Ball from Teeing Ground*). *Match Play*, If you're out of turn, you may have to replay the stroke; *Stroke Play*, if you're out of turn, you could be DISQUALIFIED.

- *Doubt as to Procedure (stroke play); Handicap Competition*
- *Provisional Ball* (Second provisional ball)

Seeing Ball

- *Searching for Ball*

Seeking a decision from the Committee

- *Discontinuance of Play; Resumption of Play*

Selection and Addition of Clubs

- *Maximum of 14 Clubs*

Sell

- *Use of Golf Skill or Reputation*

Serious breach

- *Committee* (etiquette)
- *Playing from Wrong Place*

Shaft

- <u>Straightness</u>: The shaft must be straight from the top of the grip to a point not more than 5 inches (127 mm) above the sole, measured from the point where the shaft ceases to be straight along the axis of the bent part of the shaft and the neck and/or socket.

- <u>Bending and Twisting Properties</u>: At any point along its length, the shaft must:

  (i) bend in such a way that the deflection is the same regardless of how the shaft is rotated about its longitudinal axis; and

  (ii) twist the same amount in both directions.

- <u>Attachment to Clubhead</u>: The shaft must be attached to the club-head at the heel either directly or through a single plain neck and/or socket. The length from the top of the neck and/or socket to the sole of the club must not exceed 5 inches (127 mm), measured along the axis of, and following any bend in, the neck and/or socket. <u>Exception for Putters</u>: The shaft or neck or socket of a putter may be fixed at any point in the head.

- *Clubs*
- *Damaged Clubs* (Shaft is dented)
- *Design*

Shape

- *Clubhead*

Share

- *Clubs*

Sharp edges

- *Club Face*

Side

- <u>Definition</u>: A *side* is a player, or two or more players who are partners.

- *Best-Ball and Four-Ball Match Play* (Side can choose order of play)
- *Order of Play—Match Play* (Side that has the honor)

Significant advantage

- *Playing from Wrong Place*

Signing and Returning Scorecard

- *Bogey and Par Competitions*
- *Four-Ball Stroke Play*
- *Scoring and Scorecard*
- *Stroke Play*
- *Stableford Competitions*

Single

- *Match*

Size

- *The Ball*
- *Clubhead*

Skill

- *Use of Golf Skill or Reputation*

Slow play

- *Bogey and Par Competitions*
- *Stableford Competitions*
- *Undue Delay*

Smooth sand or soil in the hazard

- *Ball in Hazard*

Snow and Ice

- Snow and ice can be <u>casual water</u> OR <u>loose impediments</u>, whichever the player chooses.

- *Manufactured Ice*

Sold by auction (players or teams)

- *Gambling*

Sole authority

- *Reinstatement of Amateur Status*

Sole of club

- *Clubhead*
- *Clubs*

Sole source of all money won

- *Gambling*

Source of money won

- *Gambling*

Specifications

- *Clubhead*
- *The Ball*

Speed of play

- <u>Playing through</u>: When a group falls one clear hole behind the group ahead, let the group behind play through. Wait until players ahead are out of range before you hit.

- <u>Search for ball</u>: Take 5 minutes to search for a ball.

Spherical Symmetry

- *The Ball*

Spike Marks

- Repair on the greens.

Spin to the ball

- *Club Face*

Spiral grip

- *Grip*

Spirit of the Rules

- *Other Conduct Incompatible with Amateurism*

Sponsor

- *Professionalism*
- *Expenses* (Sponsored Handicap Competitions)

Spoon the ball

- *Striking the Ball*

Spot from which the original ball was lifted

- *Procedure When Play Resumed*

Spot not determinable

- *Placing and Replacing*
- *Wrong Ball*

Spring

- *Club Face*

Stableford Competitions (Rule 32–1b)

- Scoring: The scoring in Stableford competitions is made by points awarded in relation to a fixed score at each hole as follows:

  Hole Played In Points

  0—More than one over fixed score or no score returned
  1—One over fixed score
  2—Fixed score
  3—One under fixed score
  4—Two under fixed score
  5—Three under fixed score
  6—Four under fixed score

- Winner: The winner is the competitor who scores the highest number of points. The marker is responsible for marking only the gross number of strokes at each hole where the competitor's net score earns one or more points.

- Maximum of 14 Clubs: Penalties applied as follows: From total points scored for the round, deduction of two points for each hole at which any breach occurred; maximum deduction per round: four points.

- One Caddie at Any One Time: Penalties applied as follows: From the points scored for the round, deduction of two points for each hole at which any breach occurred; maximum deduction per round: four points.

- Undue Delay; Slow Play: The competitor's score is adjusted by deducting two points from the total points scored for the round.

Disqualification Penalties (Rule 32–2)

- From the Competition: (Rule 32–2a) A competitor is disqualified from the competition for a breach of any of the following:

Agreement to Waive Rules
Artificial Devices and Unusual Equipment
Caddie (having more than one; failure to correct breach immediately)
Clubs
Discontinuance of Play
Handicap (playing off higher handicap; failure to record handicap)
Practice Before or Between Rounds
Refusal to Comply with Rule
Signing and Returning Scorecard
The Ball
Time of Starting and Groups
Undue Delay; Slow Play (repeated offense)
Wrong Score for Hole

- <u>For a Hole</u>: (Rule 32–2b) In all other cases where a breach of a Rule would result in disqualification, the competitor is disqualified only for the hole at which the breach occurred.

- *Bogey and Par Competitions*
- *Committee*

Stakes

- *Water Hazards*

Stance

- <u>Definition</u>: Taking the *stance* consists in a player placing his feet in position for and preparatory to making a stroke.

- After grounding your club, you have *addressed the ball*.

- You are allowed to place your feet firmly as you take a stance, but you cannot *build a stance* by standing on something, creating a mound, etc.

- *Abnormal Ground Conditions*
- *Building Stance*
- *Immovable Obstruction*
- *Improving Lie, Area of Intended Stance or Swing, or Line of Play*
- *Tee-Markers*

Stand

- Away from the person playing a stroke.

- NOT behind the player.

- NOT behind the ball.

- NOT behind the hole when the player is putting.

- *Flagstick Attended, Removed or Held Up* (Stands near flagstick)
- *In Bounds*
- *Stance*
- *Tee box* (Standing outside the tee box)
- *Teeing* (Stand outside the teeing ground)

Standard

- *The Ball*

Standing Astride or on Line of Putt (Rule 16–1e)

- <u>Must not stand astride or touching line of putt</u>: The player must not make a stroke on the putting green from a stance astride, or with either foot touching, the line of putt or an extension of that line behind the ball.

- *Putting Green*

Starting and Groups

- *Time of Starting and Groups*
- *Order of Play—Match Play*
- *Order of Play—Stroke Play*

Starting times

- *Committee*

State or regional golf association

- *Expenses*

Status While Awaiting Reinstatement

- *Reinstatement of Amateur Status*

Steel face

- *Club Face*

Stipulated Round

- <u>Definition</u>: The *stipulated round* consists of playing the holes of the course in their correct sequence unless otherwise authorized by the Committee. The number of holes in a stipulated round is 18 unless a smaller number is authorized by the Committee. As to extension of stipulated round in match play, see Rule *Winner*.

Stopped (ball)

- *By Another Ball*

- *By Opponent, Caddie or Equipment in Match Play*
- *By Outside Agency*
- *By Player, Partner, Caddie or Equipment*

Stopping play

- *Discontinuance of Play; Resumption of Play*

Straight grooves

- *Club Face*

Straightness of shaft

- *Shaft*

Striking Faces

- *Clubhead*

Striking Flagstick or Attendant

- *Ball Striking Flagstick or Attendant*
- *By Opponent, Caddie or Equipment in Match Play*

Striking the Ball (Rule 14)

- <u>Strike fairly</u>: You must strike fairly at the ball, and not use your club to scrape, hook, or spoon the ball. (Rule 14–1)

- <u>No assistance</u>: While making your stroke, you're not allowed to have physical assistance or protection from the elements (See *Assistance*). (Rule 14–2)

- <u>Striking the ball more than once</u>: If a player's club strikes the ball more than once in the course of a stroke, the player must count the stroke and add a penalty stroke, making two strokes in all. (Rule 14–4)

- *Artificial Devices and Unusual Equipment*
- *Assistance*
- *Ball Moving in Water*
- *Playing Moving Ball*
- *Striking the Ball More Than Once*

Striking the Ball More than Once (Rule 14–4)

- <u>Count two stokes</u>: If a player's club strikes the ball more than once in the course of a stroke, the player must count the stroke and add a penalty stroke, making two strokes in all.

- *Playing Moving Ball*
- *Striking the Ball*

Stroke

- <u>Definition</u>: A *stroke* is the forward movement of the club made with the intention of striking at and moving the ball, but if a player checks his downswing voluntarily before the clubhead reaches the ball he has not made a stroke.

- *Assistance* (Striking the Ball)

Stroke and distance

- *Ball Lost or Out of Bounds*
- *Provisional Ball*

Stroke Play (Rule 3)

- *Agreement to Waive Rules*
- *Artificial Devices and Unusual Equipment*
- *By Fellow-Competitor, Caddie or Equipment in Stroke Play*
- *Clubs*
- *Committee*
- *Disputes and Decisions*
- *Disqualification*
- *Doubt as to Procedure*
- *Failure to Hole Out*
- *Four-Ball Stroke Play*
- *General Penalty*
- *Handicap* (Strokes given or received)
- *Improving lie, swing, or line of play*
- *Information as to Strokes Taken*
- *Order of Play*
- *Penalty*
- *Playing from Wrong Place* (Strokes disregarded)
- *Refusal to Comply with a Rule*
- *Scoring and Scorecard*
- *Striking the ball*
- *Winner*
- *Wrong information*

Stroke table

- *Committee*

Stroke While Another Ball in Motion

- *Making Stroke While Another Ball in Motion*

Structural purposes

- *Clubhead*

Students

- *Instruction*

Submerged ball in a water hazard

- *Searching for Ball*

Submitted to Committee

- *Reinstatement of Amateur Status*

Subsequent day

- *Procedure When Play Resumed*

Substitute a ball on spot from which original ball lifted

- *Procedure When Play Resumed*

Substituted Ball (Rule 15–2)

- <u>Definition</u>: A *substituted ball* is a ball put into play for the original ball that was either in play, lost, out of bounds or lifted.

- <u>Must hole out with the ball played from the tee</u>: A player must hole out with the ball played from the teeing ground unless the ball is lost, out of bounds or the player substitutes another ball, whether or not substitution is permitted. (Rule 15–1)

- <u>A player may substitute a ball</u>: A player may substitute a ball when proceeding under a Rule that permits the player to play, drop or place another ball in completing the play of a hole. The substituted ball becomes the ball in play.

- <u>Substitutes a ball when not permitted</u>: If a player substitutes a ball when not permitted to do so under the Rules, that substituted ball is not a wrong ball; it becomes the ball in play. If the mistake is not corrected and the player makes a stroke at a wrongly substituted ball, he incurs the penalty prescribed by the applicable Rule and in stroke play, must play out the hole with the substituted ball.

- *Ball Moved in Measuring (Ball at Rest Moved)*
- *Ball Unfit for Play*
- *Playing from Wrong Place*
- *When Ball Dropped or Placed is in Play*
- *Wrong Ball*

Sudden illness

- *Discontinuance of Play; Resumption of Play*

Suggestion given to a player

- <u>Advice</u>: Any suggestion given to a golfer that might affect how he or she plays, chooses a club, or makes a stroke, is called *advice*. General information about the course or Rules is ok.

Surface Irregularities

- *Improving Lie, Area of Intended Stance or Swing, or Line of Play*

Surface of putting green

- *Testing*

Surface of the teeing ground

- *Teeing*

Surface roughness

- *Ball Unfit for Play*
- *Club Face*

Suspend play

- *Committee*
- *Discontinuance of Play; Resumption of Play*
- *Procedure When Play Suspended by Committee*

Sweepstakes

- *Gambling*

Swing

- *Abnormal Ground Conditions*
- *Improving Lie, Area of Intended Stance or Swing, or Line of Play*

Symbolic Prize

- <u>Amateur Status</u>: A *symbolic prize* is a trophy made of gold, silver, ceramic, glass or the like that is intended for display purposes only and has no significant utilitarian value.

- *Prizes*

Symmetrical cross-section

- *Club Face*

Symmetry

- *The Ball*

T

Table of handicap strokes

- *Committee*

Taking a stance

- After grounding your club, you have *addressed the ball.*

- *Addressing the Ball*
- *Improving lie, swing, or line of play*

Taking a stroke

- *Artificial Devices and Unusual Equipment*
- *Striking the ball*

Tape

- *Artificial Devices and Unusual Equipment*

Tapered

- *Grip*

Team Events

- *Expenses*

Teams

- *Advice*

Tee

- <u>Definition</u>: A *tee* is a device designed to raise the ball off the ground. It must not be longer than 4 inches (101.6 mm) and it must not be designed or manufactured in such a way that it could indicate the line of play or influence the movement of the ball.

Tee box (teeing ground)

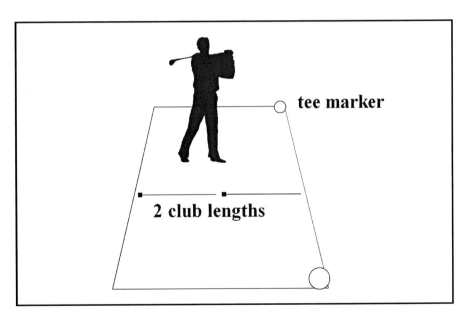

- <u>Rectangular Area</u>: A rectangle defined by two tee markers and extending two club lengths back from the direction of the green.

- <u>Outside the tee box</u>: To be outside the tee box, ALL of the ball must be outside the defined boundary.

- <u>May stand outside</u>: You may stand outside the teeing ground to play a ball that's inside the teeing ground; but, you aren't allowed to move the tee markers to help your stance or make it legally within the tee box boundaries.

- *Ball falling off the tee*
- *Improving lie, swing, or line of play*
- *Playing outside the teeing ground*
- *Second ball*

Teeing (Rule 11–1)

- When the player's ball is to be teed within the teeing ground, it must be placed on:

  (a) <u>the surface</u> of the teeing ground including an irregularity of surface (whether or not created by the player); or

  (b) <u>a tee</u> placed in or on the surface of the teeing ground; or

  (c) <u>sand</u> or other natural substance placed on the surface of the teeing ground.

- <u>Player may stand outside</u>: A player may stand outside the teeing ground to play a ball within it.

- <u>Non-conforming tee</u>: In teeing, if a player uses a non–conforming tee or any other object to raise the ball off the ground, he is DISQUALIFIED.

- *Teeing Ground*

Teeing ground (Rule 11)

- <u>Definition</u>: The *teeing ground* is the starting place for the hole to be played. It is a rectangular area two club–lengths in depth, the front and the sides of which are defined by the outside limits of two tee–markers. A ball is outside the teeing ground when all of it lies outside the teeing ground.

- *Ball Falling Off Tee*
- *Committee*
- *Playing from Outside Teeing Ground*
- *Playing from Wrong Place*
- *Tee Box*
- *Teeing*
- *Tee-markers*
- *Threesomes and Foursomes*

Tee-Markers (Rule 11–2)

- <u>Player moves tee-markers</u>: Before a player makes his first stroke with any ball on the teeing ground of the hole being played, the tee–markers are deemed to be fixed. In these circumstances, if the player moves or allows to be moved a tee–marker for the purpose of avoiding interference with his stance, the area of his intended swing or his line of play, he incurs the penalty for a breach of Rule *Ball Played As it Lies*.

- *Ball Played As it Lies*
- *Tee Box*
- *Teeing Ground*

Temporary suspension of play

- *Committee*

Terms and conditions

- *Use of Golf Skill or Reputation*

Testimonial Award

- <u>Definition</u>: A *testimonial award* is an award for notable perform-
ances or contributions to golf as distinguished from competition
prizes. A testimonial award may not be a monetary award.

- *Prizes*

Testing

- <u>Surface of putting green</u>: During the play of a hole, a player must
not test the surface of the putting green by rolling a ball or roughening or scraping the surface. (Rule 16–1d)

- <u>Condition of the hazard</u>: *Ball in a hazard*

- *Practice*
- *Practice Before or Between Rounds*
- *Putting Green*
- *The Ball*

The Ball (Appendix III)

- <u>Weight</u>: The weight of the ball must not be greater than 1.620
ounces avoirdupois (45.93 gm).

- <u>Size</u>: The diameter of the ball must not be less than 1.680 inches
(42.67 mm). This specification will be satisfied if, under its own
weight, a ball falls through a 1.680 inches diameter ring gauge in
fewer than 25 out of 100 randomly selected positions, the test being
carried out at a temperature of 23 + 1°C.

- <u>Spherical Symmetry</u>: The ball must not be designed, manufactured
or intentionally modified to have properties which differ from those
of a spherically symmetrical ball.

- <u>Initial Velocity</u>: The initial velocity of the ball must not exceed the limit specified when measured on apparatus approved by the United States Golf Association.

- <u>Overall Distance Standard</u>: The combined carry and roll of the ball, when tested on apparatus approved by the United States Golf Association, must not exceed the distance specified under the conditions set forth in the Overall Distance Standard for golf balls on file with the United States Golf Association.

- *Ball*
- *Best-Ball and Four-Ball Match Play*
- *Bogey and Par Competitions*
- *Four-Ball Stroke Play*
- *Stableford Competitions*

The Committee

- *Committee*

The Course

- *Committee*

The Player (Rule 6)

- *Ball*
- *Caddie*
- *Discontinuance of Play; Resumption of Play*
- *Handicap*
- *Rules*
- *Stroke Play*
- *Time of Starting and Groups*
- *Undue Delay; Slow Play*

The Spirit of the Game

- Etiquette: Unlike many sports, golf is played, for the most part, without the supervision of a referee or umpire. The game relies on the integrity of the individual to show consideration for other players and to abide by the Rules. All players should conduct themselves in a disciplined manner, demonstrating courtesy and sportsmanship at all times, irrespective of how competitive they may be. This is the spirit of the game of golf.

Three-Ball Match Play (Rule 30–2)

- Each player competes against each other; i.e., each player has a match against the other two players.

Ball at Rest Moved by an Opponent

- One stroke penalty: Except as otherwise provided in the Rules, if the player's ball is touched or moved by an opponent, his caddie or equipment other than during search, Rule *By Opponent, Caddie or Equipment in Match Play* applies. That opponent incurs a penalty of one stroke in his match with the player, but not in his match with the other opponent.

Ball Deflected or Stopped by an Opponent Accidentally

- No penalty: If a player's ball is accidentally deflected or stopped by an opponent, his caddie or equipment, there is no penalty. In his match with that opponent the player may play the ball as it lies or, before another stroke is played by either side, he may cancel the stroke and play a ball without penalty as nearly as possible at the spot from which the original ball was last played (see Rule *Making Next Stroke from Where Previous Stroke Made*). In his match with the other opponent, the ball must be played as it lies.

- Exception:

    a. *Ball Striking Flagstick or Attendant*
    b. *Exerting Influence on Ball* (ball purposely deflected or stopped by opponent)

- *Best-Ball and Four-Ball Match Play*
- *Match*

Threesomes and Foursomes (Rule 29)

General (Rule 29–1)

- Order of play: In a threesome or a foursome, during any stipulated round the partners must play alternately from the teeing grounds and alternately during the play of each hole. Penalty strokes do not affect the order of play.

Match Play (Rule 29–2)

- Play out of order: If a player plays when his partner should have played, his side loses the hole.

Stroke Play (Rule 29–3)

- Incorrect order: If the partners make a stroke or strokes in incorrect order, such stroke or strokes are canceled and the side incurs a penalty of two strokes. The side must correct the error by playing a ball in correct order as nearly as possible at the spot from which it first played in incorrect order (see Rule *Making Next Stroke from Where Previous Stroke Made*).

- Disqualification: If the side makes a stroke on the next teeing ground without first correcting the error or, in the case of the last hole of the round, leaves the putting green without declaring its intention to correct the error, the side is disqualified.

- *Match*

Through the Green

- Definition: *Through the green* is the whole area of the course except:

  a. The teeing ground and putting green of the hole being played; and

  b. All hazards on the course.

Ties

- *Committee*
- *Winner*

Time limit

- *Committee*
- *Disputes and Decisions*

Time of Starting and Groups (Rule 6–3)

- The player must start at the time established by the Committee.

- Remain in group: The competitor must remain throughout the round in the group arranged by the Committee unless the Committee authorizes or ratifies a change. Penalty for Breach of this rule is DISQUALIFICATION.

- Penalty for being late: The Committee may provide in the conditions of a competition that, if the player arrives at his starting point, ready to play, within five minutes after his starting time, in the absence of circumstances that warrant waiving the penalty of disqualification, the penalty for failure to start on time is loss of the first hole in match play or two strokes at the first hole in stroke play instead of disqualification.

- *Best-Ball and Four-Ball Match Play*

Touching Line of Putt (Rule 16–1a)

- Line of putt must NOT be touched except:

    (i) <u>Player may remove loose impediments</u>, provided he does not press anything down.

    (ii) <u>Player may place the club in front of the ball</u> when addressing it, provided he does not press anything down.

    (iii) <u>In measuring</u> (See *Ball Moved in Measuring*).

    (iv) <u>In lifting the ball</u> (See *Lifting and Cleaning Ball*).

    (v) <u>In pressing down a ball-marker</u>

    (vi) <u>In repairing old hole plugs or ball marks</u> on the putting green (See *Repair of Hole Plugs, Ball Marks and Other Damage*).

    (vii) <u>In removing movable obstructions</u> (See *Movable Obstruction*).

- *Loose Impediments*
- *Putting Green*
- *Standing Astride or on Line of Putt*

Towel

- *Artificial Devices and Unusual Equipment*

Training camp

- *Expenses*

Transparent material

- *Clubhead*

Traps

- DON'T ground your club.

- Rake after every shot.

- *Bunker*

Travel time

- *Expenses*

Treatment

- *Club Face*

Turf

- *Improving Lie, Area of Intended Stance or Swing, or Line of Play*

Twigs

- *Loose Impediments*

Twisting of shaft

- *Shaft*

Two grips

- *Grip*

Two or more competitors have the same score at a hole

- *Order of Play—Stroke Play*

Types of Competition

- *Bogey and Par Competitions*
- *Stableford Competitions*

U

Unacceptable Forms of Gambling

- *Gambling*

Unauthorized Attendance (Rule 17–2)

- <u>Attends flagstick without player's authority or knowledge</u>: If an opponent or his caddie in match play or a fellow–competitor or his caddie in stroke play, without the player's authority or prior knowledge, attends, removes or holds up the flagstick during the stroke or while the ball is in motion, and the act might influence the movement of the ball, the opponent or fellow–competitor incurs the applicable penalty.

- <u>Penalty for Breach of Rule</u>: *Match play*: Loss of hole; *Stroke play*: Two strokes.

- <u>Ball strikes the flagstick</u>: In stroke play if a breach of this Rule occurs and the competitor's ball subsequently strikes the flagstick, the person attending or holding it or anything carried by him, the competitor incurs no penalty. The ball is played as it lies except that, if the stroke was made on the putting green, the stroke is canceled and the ball must be replaced and replayed.

- *Flagstick*

Undue Delay; Slow Play (Rule 6–7)

- <u>Pace of play</u>: The player must play without undue delay and in accordance with any pace of play guidelines that the Committee may establish.

- <u>Between holes</u>: Between completion of a hole and playing from the next teeing ground, the player must not unduly delay play. If the player unduly delays play between holes, he is delaying the play of the next hole and the penalty applies to that hole.

- <u>Penalty for Breach of Rule</u>: *Match Play*, Loss of hole; *Stroke Play*, Two strokes.

- <u>Committee set guidelines</u>: For the purpose of preventing slow play, the Committee may, in the conditions of a competition, establish pace of play guidelines including maximum periods of time allowed to complete a stipulated round, a hole or a stroke. <u>Stroke Play</u>: The Committee may, in such a condition, modify the penalty for a breach of this Rule as follows: *First offense*, One stroke; *Second offense*, Two strokes.

- *Best-Ball and Four-Ball Match Play*
- *Bogey and Par Competitions*
- *Four-Ball Stroke Play*
- *Slow Play*
- *Stableford Competitions*
- *The Player*

Unfair advantage

- *Playing from Wrong Place*
- *Playing out of turn*

Unfit for Play

- *Ball Unfit for Play*
- *Damaged Clubs*

United States Golf Association

- *Artificial Devices and Unusual Equipment*
- *The Ball*

Unplayable

- *Ball Played Within Water Hazard*
- *Ball Unplayable*
- *Committee* (course)

Unusual Equipment

- *Artificial Devices and Unusual Equipment*

Use of Golf Skill or Reputation

- <u>No financial gain</u>: Except as provided in the Rules, an amateur golfer of golf skill or reputation must not use that skill or reputation to promote, advertise or sell anything or for any financial gain.

- <u>Lending Name or Likeness</u>: An amateur golfer of golf skill or reputation must not use that skill or reputation to obtain payment, compensation, personal benefit or any financial gain, directly or indirectly, for allowing his name or likeness to be used for the advertisement or sale of anything. An amateur golfer may accept golf equipment from anyone dealing in such equipment, provided no advertising is involved.

- <u>Personal Appearance</u>: An amateur golfer of golf skill or reputation must not use that skill or reputation to obtain payment, compensation, personal benefit or any financial gain, directly or indirectly, for a personal appearance. <u>Exception</u>: An amateur golfer may receive actual expenses in connection with a personal appearance, provided no golf competition or exhibition is involved.

- <u>Broadcasting and Writing</u>: An amateur golfer of golf skill or reputation may receive payment, compensation, personal benefit or any financial gain from broadcasting or writing, provided:

  (a) the broadcasting or writing is part of his primary occupation or career and golf Instruction is not included (Rule *Instruction*); or

  (b) the broadcasting or writing is on a part-time basis, the player is actually the author of the commentary, articles or books and Instruction in playing golf is not included.

  (c) An amateur golfer of golf skill or reputation must not promote or advertise anything within the commentary, articles or books and must not lend his name or likeness to the promotion or sale of the commentary, article or books (see *Lending Name or Likeness* above).

- <u>Grants and Scholarships</u>: An amateur golfer of golf skill or reputation must not accept the benefits of a grant or scholarship, except one whose terms and conditions have been approved by the USGA. The terms and conditions of grants and scholarships provided by schools that are members of the National Collegiate Athletic Association, the Association of Intercollegiate Athletics for Women, the National Association for Intercollegiate Athletics, the National Junior College Athletic Association or other similar organizations governing athletes at academic institutions are approved by the USGA.

- <u>Membership</u>: An amateur golfer of golf skill or reputation must not accept an offer of membership in a golf club or privileges at a golf course, without full payment for the class of membership or privilege, if such an offer is made as an inducement to play for that club or course.

- *Amateur Status*

Used for any commercial purpose

- *Professionalism*

USGA

- *Artificial Devices and Unusual Equipment*
- *Committee*
- *Disputes and Decisions*
- *Gambling*
- *Prizes* (Policy on Gambling)
- *Procedure for Enforcement of the Rules*
- *The Ball*
- *Use of Golf Skill or Reputation*

V

Value

- *Prizes*

Velocity

- *The Ball*

W

Wagering

- *Gambling*

Waist

- *Grip*

Waiting period

- *Reinstatement of Amateur Status*

Waive right to any prize money

- *Gambling*
- *Prizes*
- *Professionalism*
- *Reinstatement of Amateur Status*

Waive Rules

- *Agreement to Waive Rules*
- *Committee*

Water (on green)

- *Abnormal Ground Conditions* (diagram "puddle on green")

Water Hazards (Rule 26)

- <u>Definition</u>: A *water hazard* is any sea, lake, pond, river, ditch, surface drainage ditch or other open water course (whether or not containing water) and anything of a similar nature on the course. All ground or water within the margin of a water hazard is part of the water hazard. The margin of a water hazard extends vertically upward and downward.

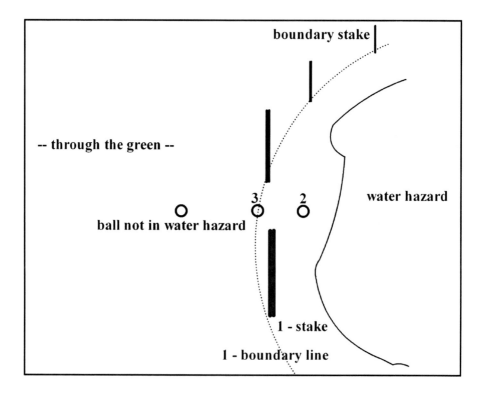

- <u>Stakes and lines</u>: Stakes and lines defining the margins of water hazards are [1—in the hazards]. Such stakes are obstructions. A ball is in a water hazard when it [2—lies in] or [3—any part of it touches the water hazard]. Stakes or lines used to define a water hazard must be <u>yellow</u>. (<u>Red</u> stakes mark lateral water hazards.) When both stakes and lines are used to define water hazards, the [1—stakes identify the hazard] and the [1—lines define the hazard margin].

- <u>Environmentally-sensitive area</u>: The Committee may make a Local Rule prohibiting play from an environmentally–sensitive area defined as a water hazard.

- *Ball Lost in Obstruction*
- *Ball Lost or Out of Bounds*
- *Ball Moving in Water*
- *Ball Played Within Water Hazard* (Rule 26–2)
- *Immovable Obstruction*
- *Procedure When Play Resumed*
- *Provisional Ball*
- *Relief for Ball in Water Hazard* (Rule 26–1)
- *Searching for Ball*

Wear of clubs

- *Clubs*

Weather

- *Artificial Devices and Unusual Equipment* (measure conditions)
- *Discontinuance of Play; Resumption of Play*

Weight

- *Clubs*
- *The Ball*

When Ball Dropped or Placed is in Play (Rule 20-4)

- <u>Ball in play when dropped</u>: If the player's ball in play has been lifted, it is again in play when dropped or placed. A <u>substituted ball</u> becomes the ball in play when it has been dropped or placed.

- *Lifting ball incorrectly substituted, dropped or placed*
- *Lifting the Ball, Dropping, and Placing*
- *Substituted Ball*

When to drop

- *Dropping and Re-Dropping*

Where Previous Stroke Made

- *Making Next Stroke from Where Previous Stroke Made*

Where to drop

- *Dropping and Re-Dropping*

Width

- *Club Face* (grooves)

Wind

- Is NOT an *outside agency.*

- *Procedure When Play Resumed*

Winner

Match Play (Rule 2–3)

- <u>Leads by more holes left to play</u>: A match is won when one side leads by a number of holes greater than the number remaining to be played.

- <u>Tie</u>: If there is a tie, the Committee may extend the stipulated round by as many holes as are required for a match to be won.

- *Match Play*

Stroke Play (Rule 3–1)

- <u>Fewest strokes</u>: The competitor who plays the stipulated round or rounds in the fewest strokes is the winner.

- <u>Handicap competition</u>: In a handicap competition, the competitor with the lowest net score for the stipulated round or rounds is the winner.

- *Stableford Competitions*
- *Stroke Play*

Withdrawing a concession

- *Concession of Next Stroke, Hole or Match*

Within the tee box

- *Playing from Outside Teeing Ground*

Within Water Hazard

- *Ball Played Within Water Hazard*

Wooden clubs

- *Club Face*

Woods

- *Clubhead*
- *Clubs*

Worms

- *By Outside Agency*
- *Loose Impediments*

Wrapped around the grip

- *Artificial Devices and Unusual Equipment*

Wrapped grip

- *Grip*

Writing

- *Use of Golf Skill or Reputation*

Written instruction

- *Instruction*

Written notice

- *Procedure for Enforcement of the Rules*

Written or oral agreement with a professional agent or sponsor

- *Professionalism*

Wrong Ball (Rule 15–3)

- Definition: A *wrong ball* is NOT the player's:

  1. Ball in play,
  2. Provisional ball, or
  3. Second ball played under Rule *Doubt as to Procedure* or Rule *Playing from Wrong Place* in stroke play;

But IS:

  1. another player's ball,
  2. an abandoned ball, and
  3. the player's original ball when it is no longer in play.

- Ball in play: Ball in play includes a ball substituted for the ball in play whether or not the substitution is permitted.

Match Play

- Loss of Hole: If a player makes a stroke at a wrong ball that is not in a hazard, he loses the hole.

- No penalty in a hazard: There is no penalty if a player makes a stroke at a wrong ball in a hazard. Any strokes made at a wrong ball in a hazard do not count in the player's score.

- Replace ball to original spot: If the wrong ball belongs to another player, its owner must place a ball on the spot from which the wrong ball was first played.

- Player and opponent exchange balls: If the player and opponent exchange balls during the play of a hole, the first to make a stroke at a wrong ball that is not in a hazard, loses the hole; when this cannot be determined, the hole must be played out with the balls exchanged.

- *Best-Ball and Four-Ball Match Play*
- *Substituted Ball*

Stroke Play

- <u>Not in a Hazard</u>: If a competitor makes a stroke or strokes at a wrong ball that is not in a hazard, he incurs a penalty of two strokes.

- <u>In a Hazard</u>: There is no penalty if a competitor makes a stroke at a wrong ball in a hazard. Any strokes made at a wrong ball in a hazard do not count in the competitor's score.

- <u>Disqualification</u>: The competitor must correct his mistake by playing the correct ball or by proceeding under the Rules. If he fails to correct his mistake before making a stroke on the next teeing ground, or in the case of the last hole of the round, fails to declare his intention to correct his mistake before leaving the putting green, he is DISQUALIFIED.

- <u>Competitor</u>: Strokes made by a competitor with a wrong ball do not count in his score. If the wrong ball belongs to another competitor, its owner must place a ball on the spot from which the wrong ball was first played.

- *Four-Ball Stroke Play*
- *Lie of ball*
- *Spot not determinable*
- *Substituted Ball*

Wrong Information

- <u>Match Play</u>: In match play, if you give wrong information to an opponent about the number of strokes you've taken, it's important to correct the error before your opponent takes the next stroke. If you don't correct the information before the next stroke, you'll lose the hole. If the hole is finished and you give wrong information that might affect your opponent's understanding of the hole's result, correct your error before anyone tees off from the next hole. If you do, there's no penalty. If someone tees off (or on the last hole, if everyone leaves the putting green) and you haven't corrected the error, you lose the hole.

- *Doubt as to Procedure, Disputes and Claims*
- *Information as to Strokes Taken*
- *Match Play*
- *Playing out of turn*

Wrong Place

- *Dropping and Re-Dropping*
- *Playing from Wrong Place*
- *Substituted Ball*

Wrong Putting Green (Rule 25–3)

- <u>Definition</u>: A *wrong putting green* is any putting green other than that of the hole being played. Unless otherwise prescribed by the Committee, this term includes a practice putting green or pitching green on the course.

- <u>Interference</u>: Interference by a wrong putting green occurs when a ball is on the wrong putting green. Interference to a player's stance or the area of his intended swing is not, of itself, interference under this Rule.

Relief

- <u>Must not play ball as it lies</u>: If a player's ball lies on a wrong putting green he must not play the ball as it lies. He must take relief, without penalty, as follows:

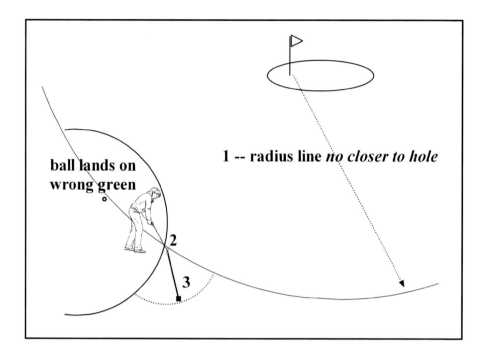

The player must [3—lift the ball and drop it within one club-length] [1—of and not nearer the hole] than the [2—nearest point of relief]. The nearest point of relief must not be in a hazard or on a putting green. When dropping the ball within one club-length of the nearest point of relief, the ball must first strike a part of the course at a spot that avoids interference by the wrong putting green and is not in a hazard and not on a putting green. The ball may be cleaned when lifted under this Rule.

- <u>Penalty for Breach of Rule</u>: *Match play,* Loss of hole; *Stroke play,* Two strokes.

- *Abnormal Ground Conditions*

Wrong Score for Hole

- *Bogey and Par Competitions*
- *Disputes and Decisions*

- *Four-Ball Stroke Play*
- *Stroke Play*
- *Stableford Competitions*

Wrongly substituted ball

- *Ball Moved in Measuring* (Ball at Rest Moved)
- *Ball Unfit for Play*

X, Y, Z

Yellow stakes or lines

- Defines boundary of a WATER HAZARD.

- Stakes and lines are part of the hazard.

- *Water Hazards*

Your ball

- *Identifying your ball*